TREES IN THE LIFE OF
THE MAYA WORLD

TREES IN THE LIFE OF THE
MAYA WORLD

Regina Aguirre de Riojas
Elfriede de Pöll

BRIT
PRESS

Botanical Research Institute of Texas

© Copyright 2007 Regina Aguirre de Riojas
ISBN13 978-1-889878-18-8

Creation and production:
Regina Aguirre de Riojas

Investigation, adviser and botanical illustrations:
Elfriede de Pöll Ph.D.

Introduction chapter text:
Igor Castillo

Advisers and reviewers:
Richard F. Fisher Ph.D., Margaret Dix Ph.D., Jeannette Ruiz Ph.D.

English translation:
Agneta Eikelenboom, Diana de Padilla, Sally Evans

Translation and proofreading:
Bárbara Balchir de Koose

Photography:
Ricardo Mata, Peter Rockstroh, Mario Madriz, Juan Ortiz, Regina de Riojas, Didier Boremanse, Mary Richardson Miller

Collaboration:
Biologist Cynthia Ralda de Recinos, Biologist AnaLu MacVean, Biologist Jaime Viñals, Ing. Luis Felipe Méndez, Wilson Castañeda, Marie Claire Paiz Msc., Agustín Estrada Monroy (†), Mark Landers Msc., Ing. Rolando Zanotti, Roberto Flores Msc, Biologist Marco Vinicio Centeno, Jorge Luján Ph.D., Luis Luján Ph.D. (†), Arch. Antonio Prado Cobos, Warren Evans Ph.D., Texas A & M University, Universidad del Valle

Former UWC students:
Lilian Márquez Forestry Engineer Ph.D.(candidate), Lic. Ricardo Ajiataz, Lic. Moisés Mérida, Walter Mérida Ph.D., Alex Guerra Noriega Msc.

Design:
Regina Batres de Porras, Silvia Quel / Quelsa

Translated from "Guauhitemala: Lugar de Bosques," Volumes I, II, III, IV, V & VI.

Editor:
Barney Lipscomb
Botanical Research Institute of Texas
509 Pecan Street
Fort Worth, Texas 76102-4060, USA

Trees in the Life of the Maya World (Regina Aguirre de Riojas and Elfriede de Pöll)

Dust Jacket image:
Sunset in the Maya Biosphere, Tikal, Guatemala. Photography by Ricardo Mata.

Published and Distributed by:
Botanical Research Institute of Texas
509 Pecan Street
Fort Worth, Texas 76102-4060, USA
Telephone: 1-817-332-4441
Fax: 1-817-332-4112
Website: www.brit.org

Botanical Research Institute of Texas
Prepress Production in Guatemala
Printed in Korea

BRIT
PRESS

The BRIT Press seeks innovation and excellence in preparation, manufacture and distribution of botanical research and scientific discoveries for the twenty-first century.
The BRIT Press – bringing out the best in botanical science for plant conservation and education.

TREES IN THE LIFE OF THE MAYA WORLD

The contribution of many people was essential for this book. We thank them for it and for sharing with us a desire to accomplish a better future through promoting the appreciation and conservation of trees. Among them, we particularly thank: Margaret Dix Ph.D., Richard F. Fisher Ph.D. and Jeannette Ruiz Ph.D.

Proceeds from this book are for education and environmental protection.
Asociación Becaria Guatemalteca
United World Colleges

TABLE OF CONTENTS

Guauhitemala, Land of Forests

Guauhitemala comes from the náhuatl term meaning "land of forests" or "place of forests." The náhuatl tribes originated in Mexico and arrived in Southern Mexico and Central América together with the Spaniards during the Conquest. The area in those days covered what had been the region occupied by the Maya civilization, known as Mesoamérica. The name Guauhitemala was given to it because most of the land was covered with forests. According to renowned historian Adrian Recinos, translator of the Popol Vuh, the name for Guatemala may have originated from this word.

Guauhitemala "Land of Forests" is a seed of hope that is sprouting in fertile soil. It is a call for attention to our heritage. The project is the result of the work of people who love nature and long for a better world. We want to give future generations a fully developed area, where all people may live in dignity and can enjoy their beautiful and privileged surroundings.

The Guauhitemala project has two objectives. The first is to serve as a well-documented work that contains information about the species of trees growing in the region, paying special attention to endangered species and their propagation. The second is to raise funds for scholarships, which the Guatemalan Scholarship Association awards to talented children who would otherwise be unable to fully develop their special abilities. This educational and cultural organization also represents the United World Colleges in Guatemala. The colleges are international communities in which young people of different nationalities, races or creeds study together, promoting peace through education. In them, special attention is given to the proper care of the environment and to social work in a number of communities.

We would like to express our sincere appreciation to all the people who invested their time and energy in this project, and to give special thanks to our sponsors. Thousands of trees and children will be forever grateful to you.

GUAUHITEMALA
"LUGAR DE BOSQUES"

Introduction

The thought of doing an English version of a book about trees in the Maya area began about ten years ago. After studying and planting these trees during all this time, I have learned of their importance in the history and development of this fantastic civilization.

Due to differences in climate and geography, we live in an area that has many different ecosystems. As a result of this, we find tremendous richness in biodiversity and one of the greatest floras in the world.

During our culture's development, we have performed some activities that have led to undesirable changes and have destroyed natural resources. In consequence, we have reduced the usefulness of some of these resources, in some cases as important as water, which is essential for life on Earth.

Often, instead of ensuring the highest possible productivity and securing a sustainable yield of these benefits, a lot of poverty has been created.

One of the reasons for writing this book is to save these natural resources as a priority for the welfare of humanity and to help the inhabitants of these areas, covered once mainly by forests, to obtain a better standard of living.

This document presents botanical data on several tree species, as well as descriptions of their ecological needs and propagation methods. Special attention is given to their native, traditional and commercial uses; each chapter is divided according to these uses. I have also included literature written about trees by different poets and authors. I hope you enjoy reading it.

I want to thank all the professionals who have contributed with the realization of this book, created mainly to make people aware of the treasure we are losing and to take action to preserve it. Without their support it would have been impossible. I would also like to thank my husband, family and friends for their support. People must understand the cycle of life. We are not going to be in this world forever. The good things you leave behind are what will survive in the future. If we plant an excellent seed with love today, tomorrow we will have greener forests and a brighter future.

Regina Aguirre de Riojas

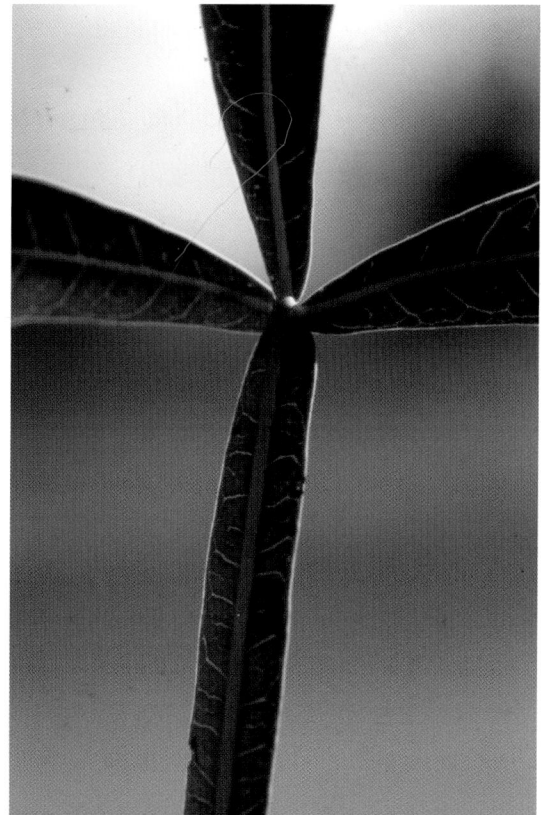

Trees in the life of the Maya World

Trees in the life of the Maya World

Maya civilization flourished in the region known archeologically as Mesoamérica (an area that today includes most of Central América and Southern Mexico). This extraordinary culture reached its peak between the sixth and ninth centuries AD, with a history covering three millennia.

Mesoamérica is a land of contrasts. Within a relatively small geographic area, the region has coasts on the Atlantic and Pacific Oceans, includes tropical lowlands and is traversed by high mountain chains. Its ever-changing topography hosts diverse ecosystems and forests. The highlands consist mainly of humid montane forests, commonly known as cloud forests. The predominant forest type in the lowland Caribbean region is humid and very humid tropical. In other areas, the landscape becomes an almost desert-like, subtropical scrub; while the lowlands consist primarily of hot, very humid tropical forest. The variety of trees is extraordinary. It is believed that the first inhabitants of the region settled on the fertile Pacific coast and were related to the cultures of Central Mexico. The Maya civilization flourished centuries later in the northern lowlands of Petén, in Guatemala, expanding into Belize, Honduras, El Salvador and Southern Mexico. Today, the vast jungle of the Maya World is still lush and plentiful, although large tracts have been cleared by illicit logging operations, and it is home to a wide variety of flora and fauna. The ancient Maya respectfully accepted the gifts provided by their surroundings, and among dense tropical jungles they built colossal cities of pyramids that served as religious and civic centers. They were advanced in mathematics, writing and astronomy. Among their many accomplishments, they applied the concept of zero long before other civilizations and developed a calendar almost as exact as the one we use today. They had complex religious, social and political structures, and they maintained commercial and diplomatic relations with faraway lands. The Maya cultivated areas surrounding their cities; themes of Nature were frequently reflected in their arts, adopted in the names of places and people, and worshipped in rituals. Among ancient cultures, the Maya were outstanding for their harmonious relationship with Earth, and the importance given to forests is manifested by their choice of the tree as the symbol for the Maya concept of the world, of Life.

Today, ethnic Maya still inhabit the same regions as in the past, significantly in Guatemala (where they represent more than half the population) and in the Mexican states of Chiapas, Campeche, and Quintana Roo. While continuing many of their ancient customs, they are also a vibrant, living force in the modern world. The trees and forests of their ancestors, however, are rapidly diminishing. Seventy-five percent of the fuel used in rural areas comes from wood, leading to large areas being deforested. At the same time, international demand for hardwoods has led to huge tracts of tropical jungle being cleared. Lack of development, along with rising population and economic needs, are depriving Mesoamérica of the forests so needed in the world and so integral to the lives of its inhabitants. Perhaps an increased knowledge of the ways of the ancient Maya and of the forests that they so depended on and respected, can help us gain a greater appreciation of what remains.

THE SACRED TREE

On earthly paradise,
Stood the tree of life.
There was no sin,
There was no death.
Its leaves would not fall,
They would not wither.

Humberto Akabal

Trees in the Popol Vuh

The ancient Maya conceived creation as a marvelous tree: the Tree of Life, Tree of the World (Wacah Chan). This mystic symbol united the three levels of the Maya cosmos, and its strongest branches marked the cardinal points, each ruled by specific forces. The Wacah Chan was the pillar that sustained the universe. The malignant Lords of Darkness dwelled among its roots and the mighty Heart of Sky lived over its crown. The trunk was the link between Earth and Man, and the Upper and Underworlds.

Trees in the Popol Vuh

Although the Tree of Life had no material presence, the Maya pictured it as a ceiba and often represented it in their religious art as well as in their architecture. The ceiba was the most sacred of all trees; its symbol, still used in indigenous textiles, represents nobility and power. It is one of the largest and most impressive trees of the region, and today the ceiba is the national tree of Guatemala, with people still believing in the divine protection of its shade. For this reason it decorates the central squares of many towns and gives its name to many others. Native to the lowlands, it is an awesome sight as it stands silhouetted against a tropical sunset.

Many other trees have sacred connotations. In the Popol Vuh, ancient stories of the Maya-K'iche', there are numerous references to the forests. This literary treasure was written after the Spanish conquest, yet it carries an ancient oral tradition that expresses an ancestral vision of creation. Its legends describe a magic world where Nature has the central role.

The importance of trees is clear from the beginning of this Sacred Book: the forests are conceived by the Creators during the formation of the world:

"By their genius alone, by their cutting edge alone, they conceived the mountain-plain, on which grew instant groves of cypress and pine." The K'iche' nation has lived in the Guatemalan western highlands for many centuries. The word "K'iche'" means many trees. Pines and cypresses are native and plentiful in these mountains, thus, in the Popol Vuh, they are the first trees specifically named, linked directly to the beginning of life.

Once the forests were created, the Creators made the animals:

> *"Why should there merely be rustling beneath the trees and bushes?"*
> *"Indeed, they had better have guardians," the other replied.*

So the creatures were formed to dwell and watch over the forest. But the animals had no language, they merely screamed in different ways, so the Creators decided to create Man. They first tried to form him out of clay and did not succeed: he had neither strength nor comprehension, and dissolved when touched by water. Then, through an oracle of Tzité seeds, they were advised to make Man out of wood. Man was carved from the strong Tzité (Palo de Pito) and Woman shaped from a flexible reed called Tzibaj. These people multiplied, but were ungrateful and never spoke to the Creators, who then sent a flood that forced them to climb the trees. In time, they became monkeys. The myth explains with colorful eloquence the resemblance between human and ape.

CEIBA
(Kapok)

.... and the first white tree arose in the north,
and the arch of the sky arose;
the first black tree came,
and the first yellow tree
and the great Mother Ceiba arose,
amidst the memories of
the destruction of the earth;
she sat down, very straight,
and raised her crown
requesting eternal leaves.

And with her branches and
her roots she called to her lord.

The Book of Chilam Balam

Botanical name:

Ceiba pentandra (L.) Gaertn.

Family:

Bombacaceae

Synonyms:

Bombax pentandrum L.

Ceiba anfractuosa (DC.) M. Gómez

Ceiba casearia Medik.

Eriodendron anfractuosum DC.

Eriodendron occidentale Don

Common names:

Ceiba, Bongo, Ceibo, Jazché, Pochota, Árbol de algodón, Ceiba de lana, Yaxché, Kapok, Silk cotton tree

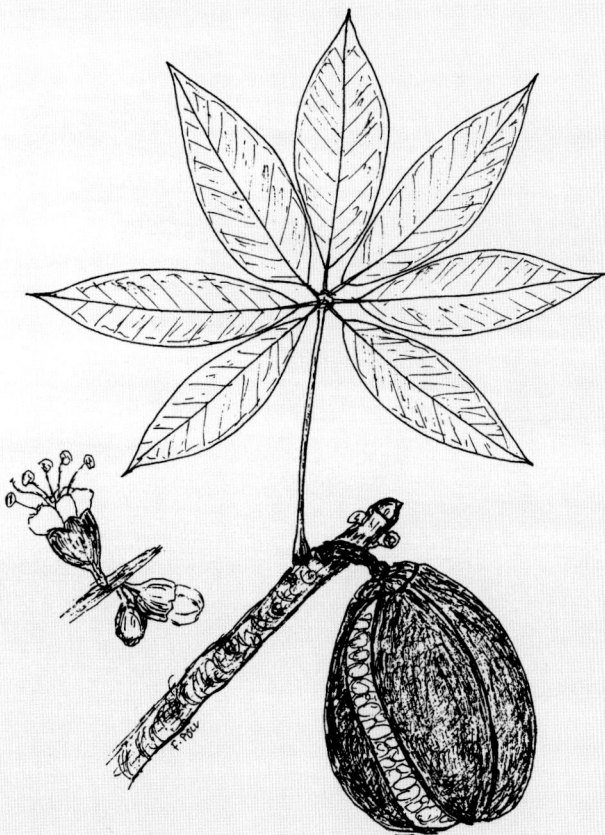

The Ceiba in Traditional Lore:

The Maya considered the ceiba as their sacred tree of life; the axis of their world. Its massive roots held the Earth together. Xibalba's domain, the Underworld, was located in its base roots. The heart of Heaven and its deities lived on the four main branches of the tree; each of these branches represented a cardinal point: White, north; red, east; yellow, south; and black, west. The indigenous races have also allocated the ceiba in a special place in their hearts, as is stated in the Sacred Manuscripts.

The ceiba represented wisdom and was linked to magical rites; it is also portrayed with distinction in hand-woven native textiles. The ceiba is intimately linked to the traditions and customs of the Maya-K'iche' people.

The most renowned ceibas in Guatemala are located in Palín, Sacapulas and Amatitlán; that of Amatitlán's Plaza is famous because it was planted 450 years ago by Brother Domingo Martínez.

In 1935, Dr. Sixto Padilla, a Salvadorean, suggested that the ceiba should be named the national tree, and later, Ulises Rojas, a Guatemalan botanist, formally proposed this. However, not until March 8, 1955, was *Ceiba pentandra* declared the National Tree of Guatemala, by presidential decree.

Ceiba tree.

Description:

The ceiba is a tree of rapid growth: its straight, perfectly round trunk can reach up to 70 meters in height and 2 meters in diameter. The widespread basal roots provide great support. The young trunk and new branches are covered with thorns, and the bark is a smooth grey-pink. The crown is wide and rounded, with very few thick branches extending horizontally. The palmately compound leaves resemble fingers. Its fruits are hard, elongated capsules that contain cotton-like fibers. This tree grows naturally from Mexico to Brazil.

Cultivated species can be found in Asia, where they are used industrially, especially in Indonesia, Thailand and Pakistan. In the Américas, Brazil is the only country that cultivates the ceiba commercially.

Ecological Requirements:

The ceiba must have a torrid tropical climate, with between 1000 and 1500 mm annual rainfall. There should also be a short dry season. It can thrive from sea level up to 500 m.

In Guatemala, this species has spread naturally in the warm and humid areas, usually growing in humid or very humid, warm sub-tropical forests in the north and in the south of the country.

Propagation:

This tree can be planted by seed or by cuttings, and can be grafted. The seed is harvested from mid-February to the end of April, and can be planted in seedbeds or growbags. If the soil is sufficiently moist, the seeds may be sown directly. For propagation by cuttings, it is preferable to choose mature vertical branches.

Planting:

The ceiba should be planted with 8 to 10 meters between each plant. It needs very little care.

Production:

Trees grown from seeds planted directly into the soil may begin to produce fibers after 5 years. Trees propagated by grafts and cuttings may begin to produce after 2 years. The harvest usually begins with 100 fruits and can produce up to an average of 700. A ceiba plantation can produce up to 450 Kg of kapok per hectare and can be productive for approximately 60 years.

Main Uses:

The most important product of the ceiba is the floss, commonly called kapok, contained in its fruits. This fiber is popularly used in pillows, mattresses, life jackets, and upholstery. Ceiba wood is very lightweight and is used for canoes, rafts, lifeboats, veneer, model airplanes, carved wood, thermal and acoustic insulation, handicrafts, paper, match boxes, and crates.

This well-loved tree can be found in many plazas and parks.

Oil from the seeds may be used in cooking, in lamps, and to make glue and soap. The leaves, rich in protein, are excellent fertilizers, and bran from the seeds is a food source. Young fruits may be eaten. The leaves and bark may be used as a tea in home remedies, as a relief for cramps, and as emetics and diuretics. From the trunk, a sap helpful in curing intestinal ailments can be obtained.

Cotton, fruit and trunk of ceiba.

PINO
(Pine)

Nothing but a prodigy,
only magical art
brought about the formation
of the mountains and the valleys;
and at once
groves of cypress and pine
burgeoned on the surface.

Popol Vuh

Botanical name:

Pinus spp.

Family:

Pinaceae

Common names:

Pino.

Pine.

The Pino in Traditional Lore:

The pine tree has, according to the Popol Vuh, existed in the Maya area ever since the Creation. Its seeds have been dispersed to other parts of the world. As an example, Central América is one of three principal regions of pine diversity. The Caribbean pine, which is the most widespread tropical species owing to its rapid growth and adaptability to hot climates, constitutes one of the biggest reserves of raw material for industrial purposes.

About sixteen species of pine are found in Mesoamérica. In Guatemala they grow in all the departments of the country, but predominantly in the mountainous areas.

Description:

Pines are resinous trees with straight trunks, whose different levels of branches give them a pyramidal shape. The rugged bark is usually covered with scales. Pines have needles borne in distinct groups, with two to five needles to a group, depending on the species. The pine family belongs to the conifers, or gymnosperms, together with the araucaria and cypress families. Conifers do not have flowers or true fruits, but seeds borne by female cones. Male cones produce pollen. All pine species are quite similar, varying only in botanical characteristics such as the number of needles held by a group, their shape, the appearance and size of cones and seeds, etc. Depending on their age and species, pine trees provide white, pink, or red wood.

Ecological Requirements:

Pines have adapted to different kinds of climates. A few species grow in hot, tropical areas at altitudes less than 1000 meters above sea level (*Pinus caribaea*). Other species have adapted to the lower montane regions, at altitudes of 1000 to 2000 meters. Still others grow in the temperate regions at high elevations (from 2000 meters up to the timberline, approximately 4000 meters). Most of the species are adapted to semi-humid conditions with 1000 mm of precipitation per year, and a long dry season.

Others grow well in semi-arid regions where annual rainfall is between 250 and 800 mm. All pines require well-drained soil. They will grow well in poor, sandy, rocky or shallow soils, where broad-leaved trees may not prosper. The soil pH may range from very acidic to alkaline, but acidic soils are preferred by most species.

Propagation:

All pine trees are seed propagated. The seeds vary according to the species. One kilogram may contain anywhere from 1000 to 2000 seeds. Seeds stored in a sealed container under refrigeration retain embryo viability for many years. To obtain a good germination rate the seeds are soaked in cold water for one day, and refrigerated at 4° or 5° C for 2 or 3 days. Then they are scattered on seedbeds of disinfected sand so that there will be 600 to 700 seedlings per square meter. The seeds are covered with a thin layer of sand, and they will take from 8 to 20 days to germinate. Young pine seedlings are very sensitive to moisture, which may cause them to "damp off" (to wither and die because of mildew); therefore, the seedbed should not be watered excessively. In 2 to 3 months' time, when the seedlings have 4 leaves, they can be transplanted to small plastic bags. Generally, the soil used for transplanting is taken from a pine forest where mycorrhiza is present. (Mycorrhiza is a beneficial relationship between fungi and the root cells of higher green plants, which is necessary for optimum growth of some plants.) After 12 to 15 months, when the pine seedlings measure 20 to 30 centimeters in height, they are ready to be planted in the field.

Planting:

In poor soils, pine seedlings are planted 2 meters apart; in fertile soils, they are planted up to 3.5 meters from each other. The terrain must be kept weed-free during the first two years. Small and weak trees are eventually thinned out to allow the bigger ones to grow, and the lower branches of healthy trees are trimmed. Seeds should be selected from a known source, so as to prevent the stand having unfavorable characteristics.

Production:

In plantations for wood production, thinning out occurs from the fifth year onward. Half the trees are taken out every time, so that between 200 and 400 trees per hectare are left after the third and last thinning. The stand is harvested after 20 to 80 years, depending on how quickly the trees grow. Production varies between 5 and 20 cubic meters of wood per hectare, per year. For fast-growing species, such as the Petén pine (*Pinus caribaea*), an annual production of 40 cubic meters of wood per hectare is possible. Pines are the most suitable trees for wood production on poor soils.

Pine trees can be attacked by caterpillars, white ants, aphids, leaf-eating ants, beetles, borers, etc. In the nursery, they are particularly sensitive to fungi that cause damping off of the seedlings during, or shortly after germination (*Pythium*). The *Armillaria* and *Phaeolus* fungi cause the roots of adult trees to rot, and fungi of the *Cronartrium* genus Pine rust.

Main Uses:

Pine wood is light and easy to work: it is used for construction, carpentry, furniture manufacture, pulp and paper, and many other things. The straight and flexible trunks are suitable for making flagstaffs and masts. The wood needs to be treated to prevent rot or damage by termites. The waste material which is left after trimming and thinning is excellent firewood. "Ocote" is a very resinous pine wood, used for starting fires. Turpentine and rosin, two valuable commercial products, are manufactured from pine resin.

Essential oils, used in medicine and perfumery, are extracted from the needles of several species; and pine cones and needles are used to decorate and aromatize houses and crafts. From the bark of some species colorants are extracted, which are useful for tanning hides. Apart from the planting of pine trees for wood production, rows of pines make excellent windbreaks, and as ornamental trees, they beautify any park, street or garden.

CIPRÉS

(Cypress)

Oh, cypress! the oldest,

the most true, silent and self-denying companions

I have dreamed many times,

of hiding my dark life

between the cypress forests.

That way, perhaps, they will whisper

during the silent nights

many things, many fabulous things

that they know!...

The Tree in Guatemalan poetry

Carlos Alberto Quintana

Botanical name:

Cupressus lusitanica Miller

Family:

Cupressaceae

Synonyms:

C. benthamii Klotzsch ex Endl.

C. benthamii var. *knightiana* Mast.

C. knightiana Knight & Perry ex Gordon

C. lindleyi Klotzsch ex Endl.

C. lusitanica var. *benthamii* (Endl.) Carrière

C. lusitanica var. *knightiana* Rehder

Common names:

Ciprés, Tsicap (Jacaltenango), Tzis (Huehuetenango), Quisis (Quiché), Chinchac, Paxaque, Ksis (Santa María volcano, Quetzaltenango).

Common cypress, Arizona cypress, Churchyard cypress, Blue cypress, Italian cypress.

The Ciprés in Traditional Lore:

Guatemala's history alludes to the existence of a particular cypress tree in Concepción Chiquirichapa which had died but was still standing erect. The circumference of its trunk measured 12 meters. History tells us that Pedro de Alvarado, the Spanish conqueror of Guatemala and his soldiers rested at the base of this tree on their way towards the conquest of the city now called Quetzaltenango.

Up to the year 1490, cypress forests probably covered most of the humid mountainous areas at altitudes equal to or higher than 2000 meters above sea level. Cypress trees are frequently associated with *Pinus ayacahuite* and fir trees (*Abies guatemalensis*).

The botanical name of the cypress (*Cupressus lusitanica*) implies that it comes from Portugal, where it has been cultivated since the 17th century in efforts to reforest the land, but it is a native of Mexico and Guatemala. Because of its durability, cypress wood of *Cupressus sempervirens* L. from the old world was used to construct the gateway of Constantinople and the original doors of Saint Peter's basilica in Rome. After eleven centuries of continuous use, they are still in good shape.

The cypress has a remarkable ability to adapt to different climatic conditions. It grows rapidly, and its abounding foliage spreads horizontally, for which reason it is very suitable for trimmed hedges.

The species that belong to the *Cupressus* genus are native to the temperate and subtropical regions of North and Central América, China, and the Himalayas. The cypress species that originates from Mexico and Guatemala is the one that is most widespread in the mountainous areas of the tropics. It grows at altitudes of 2200 to 3300 meters. In Guatemala it grows naturally in the departments of El Progreso (Sierra de las Minas), Jalapa, Chimaltenango, El Quiché, Totonicapán, Quetzaltenango and San Marcos. The greenest and thickest cypress forests are on the hills of

Tecpán, San Marcos and Quetzaltenango, although these are gradually being destroyed.

Description:

The cypress is an evergreen tree that grows as tall as 20 to 35 meters. Its crown can be large or small, narrow or sparse, and its trunk is straight. The leaves are scale-like and fragrant. The tiny, solitary male cones are distributed on the ends of the younger branches. The female cones are round and woody, approximately 1.5 cm in diameter. They are bluish gray at first, but when they mature they turn brown. When they dry, they open and drop numerous seeds. Cypress wood is white and compact. It has a good texture and is moderately strong and resistant to insect attack. It is very durable as long as it is kept in a sheltered place.

Ecological Requirements:

Cupressus lusitanica grows at higher elevations, from 1300 to 3300 meters above sea level. It requires 1000 to 2500 mm of rainfall per year, with a dry season of two or three months. The annual mean temperature should range from 20° to 32° C. The soil must have a medium texture and a neutral to acidic pH, and it must be deep and well-drained. Cypress does not grow in poor soils and does not endure prolonged droughts; however it tolerates shade, freezing temperatures, and salty breezes. It is found in the ecological zones called humid tropical, lower montane or montane forest.

Propagation:

The mature female cones can be picked almost year-round but the best time for gathering fruits is between August and January. The fruits are ripe when they are brown; it is preferable to cut some branches with many fruits on them and sun-dry them. They can then be preserved in a cool, dry location. No special treatment is necessary before sowing.

Planting:

Cypress must be sown during the rainy season and the ground where the trees are planted must be kept weed-free. The crowns of cypress trees quickly become very dense. It is

therefore advisable to prune them after several years, unless they are to serve as windbreaks. Seven years after planting, the trees can be thinned out for the first time; after that they can be thinned every other year. The final harvest occurs 25 to 30 years after the establishment of the tree farm.

Production:

Under favorable growing conditions and during the initial years, cypress trees grow quickly (1.5 m per year). They can produce between 15 and 40 cubic meters of wood per year per hectare.

In nurseries, cypress can be harmed by crickets and snails. In very wet places, *C. lusitanica* is susceptible to canker (*Agrobacterium tumefaciens*) and to gall-nut, also called cypress nut, which is caused by *Monochaetia unicornis* and deforms the stem.

Main Uses:

The wood of the different cypress species varies somewhat in quality, but in general it is strong and durable, used for heavy as well as light construction, the manufacture of simple furniture, and resonators for guitars and mandolins. The short fibers in cypress wood make it suitable for pulp, veneers, plywood, etc. In Guatemala, large quantities of young branches are used for decorating during special celebrations and for making wreaths. These are crafted to adorn niches and mausoleums in cemeteries, principally on All Saints' Day (Día de Todos los Santos) and the Day of the Dead (Día de los Fieles Difuntos), occurring on the first and second days of November. Cypress generates good fuel and charcoal. The bark contains astringent substances, and it, as well as the cones, has medicinal properties.

Cypress trees are often planted in rows to provide wind protection. Their dense growing habit makes them very suitable for such windbreaks and hedges. *Cupressus lusitanica* is melliferous, and, like other members of the cypress family, it is commonly planted for ornamental purposes.

PINABETE
(Guatemalan Fir)

This time let it be a tree whose roots
are so deep that in the depth of the
earth they are as claws
nailed into her bowels;
So tall, so leafy, so large
as largesse itself;
it reaches the sky, and its shadow
will shelter all humanity!

Let it be a tree never seen before,
with its branches full of hope,
and blooms of happiness,
and universal love;
a tree for future laws:
a marvelous tree of peace!
For centuries of fraternal humanity,
and good fortune on earth!
My son!
Let this Christmas tree be for all men!

The Christmas Tree
Ovidio Fernández Ríos

Botanical name:

Abies guatemalensis Rehder

Family:

Pinaceae

Synonym:

A. guatemalensis var. *tacanensis* (Lundell) Martínez

Abies tacanensis Lundell

Common names:

Pinabete, Parchac, Pacachaque, Pashaque fir, Romerillo.

Guatemalan fir.

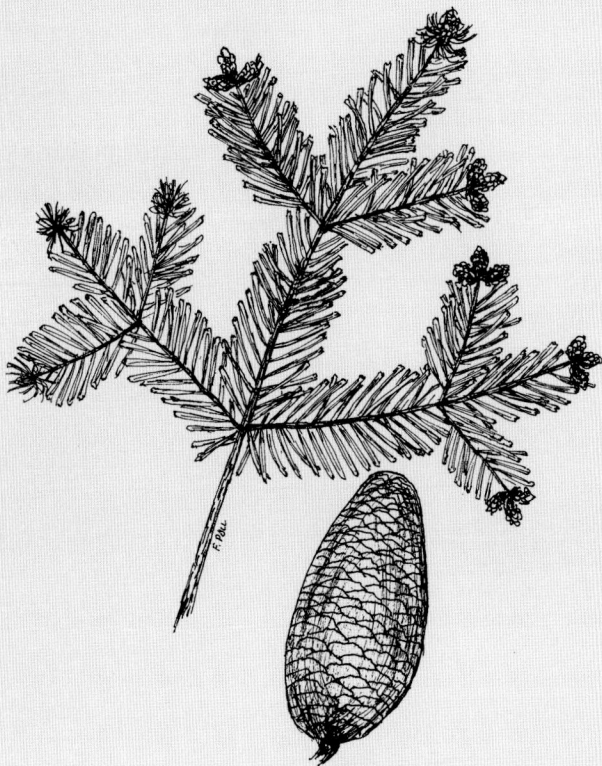

The Pinabete in Traditional Lore:

The pinabete, or Guatemalan fir, is a tree outstanding in Guatemalan traditions, especially for its marvelous fragrance. The plains of southern Mexico and Guatemala, where many conifer species were abundant, were partially razed by the migratory Maya culture before the arrival of the Spanish in the 16th century. During the Colonial era, more and more wood was needed for construction. Nevertheless, the pinabete flourished in western Guatemala until the 19th century. In the 1940s it could still be found in many locations. In 1950, large parcels of land were exploited, and at the beginning of the 1980s those with pinabetes totaled very few hectares.

Since 1941, the pinabete has been on the protected species list, and in 1979 CITES added it to the international list of endangered species.

Description:

The pinabete is an evergreen; it can grow to 45 meters high, with a trunk up to 1 meter in diameter. Its growth is symmetric. The bark, with slightly defined stained areas, is light brown, gray, dark brown or reddish; the crown, pyramidal or conical oblong. The leaves are sparse, ascending linearly, dark green and shiny on top, and silvery underneath. The leaves, which are spirally arranged on the branches even though they seem to be placed in two rows, have resiniferous canals.

The cylindrical cones are light brown, measure up to 12 cm long and have flat crossed scales. The winged seeds are light brown, shaped as an oval wedge.

In Guatemala, the pinabete tree can be found in Quiché, Chichicastenango, Sierra de Las Minas, Totonicapán, Sololá, Huehuetenango, Quetzaltenango, San Marcos and Jalapa. In Mexico, it can be found in Chiapas, Oaxaca and Guerrero.

Ecological Requirements:

The pinabete grows in the tropical cool cloud forests of the high mountains, especially at altitudes of 2700 to 3600 meters. The tree requires from 1500 to 3000 mm rainfall per year, concentrated from April to October, with some scattered rain showers during the rest of the year. A temperature of around 9° to 10° C. is ideal. At higher altitudes, the tree withstands below zero temperatures. It can also be found in soils based on volcanic ash with varying textures.

Pinabete forests are of limited extension and usually are closely associated with *Pinus ayacahuite* (White Pine), *Pinus hartwegii* and *Cupressus lusitanica*.

Propagation:

The pinabete tree reproduces by seed that is collected from October through January. Seed production is reduced if productive branches are pruned; this could be one of the reasons that this species is in danger of extinction. It has been a Guatemalan tradition to use fir branches for decoration at Christmas and large numbers were and still are routinely harvested for that purpose.

The cones open and fall to pieces on the tree when they are ripe. The best time for seed collection is when the scales are changing color, from blue or blue-green to dark green and purple; the cones should be picked with the bracts closed to avoid losing any seeds. This species has viable seeds every 2 or 3 years. Cones should be dried in the shade for 8 weeks to complete ripening.

The pinabete is very difficult to reproduce in nurseries. The best months for planting are April and May. The plant is transplanted to growbags after 4 or 5 weeks of germination; this way the pinabete can be in a nursery for up to 2 years.

Planting:

In Guatemala, most of the pinabete forests are natural and are cultivated in very few places. The tree should be planted in its definitive site when it is 2 years old. It requires semi-shaded areas, preferably under pine, and can take advantage of the mycorrhiza. Open plantations of pinabete without canopies should be protected from frost by covering the seedlings with coarse straw or shrubbery branches, at least for the first year. At three years of age, the pinabete can be combined with other crops such as corn, lima beans, green beans, peas, etc., thus making the plantation even more profitable.

Production:

After seven years growth, the pinabete can be harvested for ornamental Christmas trees. Rudimentary methods of tree harvesting, such as cutting, almost at ground level, cause the death of the tree and do not allow the use of stumps for tree regeneration.

Generally, this species is relatively free; but not immune to insect attacks.

Main Uses:

The wood is white, with pinkish to reddish tones closer to the center of the tree. It is straight, easy to split, flexible, somewhat hard, strong. The wood has limited resistance to the outdoors.

It is very popular for making looms, interior paneling, roofs for rural housing, firewood and charcoal.

The pulp of the pinabete is greatly appreciated by the paper industry. The branches are frequently cut to build temporary shelters. However its main use is decorative, especially in the Christmas season for its unique fragance.

Through an incision, the tree produces a great amount of balsamic oil that is used in medicines and paints.

PALO DE PITO
(Whistle Tree)

Draw lots with your maize kernels
and your seeds of tzité.

Do this, and one will know
whether to carve your mouth and eyes in wood.

This is what was said to the fortunetellers.
The flesh of man was made from tzité
but when woman was formed by the
Creator and the Maker,
reed mace was used to make her flesh.

These were the materials
the Creator and the Maker
wanted them to be composed of.

Popol Vuh

Botanical name:

Erythrina berteroana Urban

Family:

Fabaceae (Leguminosae)

Common names:

Palo de Pito, Miche, Machetillos, Coralillo, Tzinté (Cobán), Tzite (Quiché).
Whistle tree.

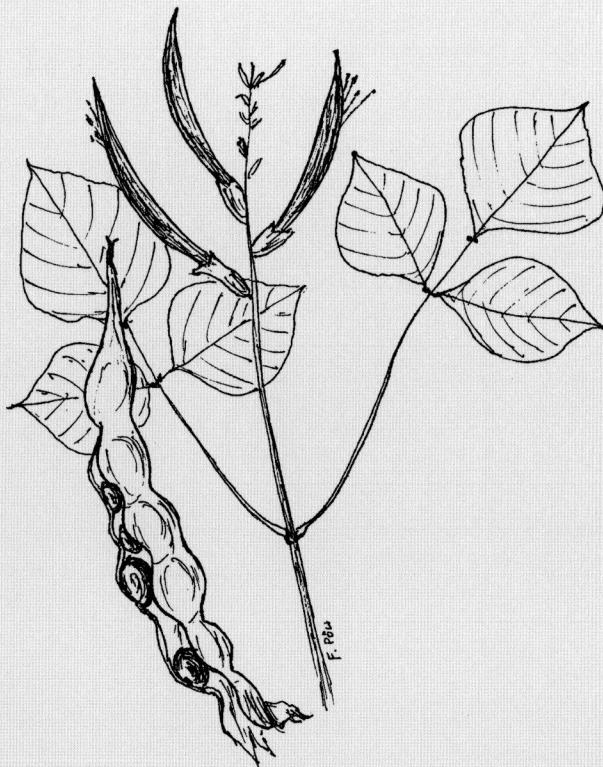

The Palo de Pito in Traditional Lore:

This tree is important in Guatemalan history because, according to the Popol Vuh, it was an ingredient in the creation of Man, and it is very significant in the magic rituals associated with the Maya-K'iche' culture. The term "Ahzite," or "Ajsite" in Q'eqchi', refers to medicine men who make magic ointments with its seeds.

In Guatemala and Honduras there is a belief that whistle tree leaves below one's pillow at night induce deep and invigorative sleep.

The Ch'orti' people of Chiquimula in eastern Guatemala plant *Erythrina berteroana* to mark the boundaries of their properties; as its petals can be made into whistles it is commonly called Palo de Pito, or "Whistle Tree."

Description:

The whistle tree is a shrub or small tree, with large, protective thorns. The leaves are composed of 3 broad leaflets, which are joined together on a long petiole. The red flowers grow in upright clusters. The fruits are short, curved pods, containing big, bright red seeds.

Ecological Requirements:

Erythrina berteroana adapts to a wide range of climates and soil types, from low elevations up to nearly 2000 meters above sea level, in humid as well as arid regions, and on heavy or poor soils. It grows in open forests in Guatemala, Honduras, El Salvador, Panama, Colombia, and the West Indies.

Propagation:

The whistle tree can be propagated by seeds or cuttings. The seeds are gathered from November to February, and they can be stored for a long time. They germinate easily, without prior treatment. Large cuttings from the vertical branches, or the tip of the main stem, work well too.

The branches from which cuttings are taken should be at least two years old and they should grow on 5 to 8 year old trees with diameters of at least 5 centimeters.

Planting:
Whistle trees are often planted along property boundaries, and they also serve as supports for climbing agricultural plants. The distance between the trees will vary with the type of crop they support.

Production:
By trimming the equivalent of one hectare every year, more than 4000 cuttings can be made for planting. The leaves and branches which are trimmed are a good source of protein for farm animals. A 400 meter hedge surrounding one hectare of pasture will produce the equivalent of 400 kg of concentrated protein annually. Many different leaf-eating insects and borers attack the tree. Whistle trees are also sensitive to certain fungi that cause the roots to rot (*Armillaria* sp., *Fomes* spp., *Corticium salmonicolor* and *Calostilbe striispora*).

Main Uses:
Erythrina berteroana has various practical uses. It fixes nitrogen in the soil; therefore, when it is intercropped with pasture, grass production improves. The foliage is a protein-rich and tasty feed for cows, goats and rabbits, or it can be used as a fertilizer.

The tree is also used for windbreaks and hedges, and for giving support to climbing crops such as black pepper and vanilla.

Dry whistle tree wood is quite soft. It is suitable for making tools, chairs, and decorative objects. It is not appropriate for fuel or for making charcoal.

The flowers, leaves, and young shoots are edible; they are delicious in soups and sauces. The seeds are poisonous, and alkaloids are extracted from the seeds of several species.

These substances serve as active ingredients in organic insecticides and rodenticides. The seeds are also made into beads for necklaces and bracelets. Nevertheless they are extremely toxic.

The bark and twigs have medicinal properties. A tea made from its shoots relieves pain and induces sleep. A yellow dye, used for coloring textiles, can be obtained from the bark.

Other Species:
Erythrina glauca Willd. Tall tree with attractive, light orange flowers. Grows in humid, lowland forests, or in swampy places below 700 meters above sea level. It is planted as a shade tree on coffee farms.

Erythrina guatemalensis Krukoff. Small tree with bright red flowers. It grows from 1200 to 1600 meters above sea level, especially in the department of Alta Verapaz, where it is native. Its characteristics and uses are similar to those of *E. berteroana*.

Erythrina poeppigiana (Walp.) O.F. Cook. Tall tree with bright orange flowers, native to South América. It has become naturalized in some regions of Costa Rica and Guatemala. It is planted as a shade tree in coffee and cocoa plantations. Also called "foreign whistle tree."

Erythrina crista-galli L. Shrub or small tree native to Brazil, with very beautiful, big, dark red flowers. In Guatemala, it is planted as an ornamental.

Erythrina berteroana. Seeds.

On the third attempt, man was successfully made of corn, the most basic and cherished food of the Maya. The cultivation of this grain was indeed essential to the development of their civilization. Ancient wisdom reaffirms a scientific premise: We are what we eat.

Another part of the Maya-K'iche' book, the Popol Vuh, narrates how the lords of darkness killed two great heroes and hung the head of one of them on a tree which was instantly covered with fruits... Calabash Tree came to be its name and much was said about it, for a princess went to see it and the hero's head split on her hand and she became pregnant. Her father, furious, ordered her execution and asked for her heart as proof. To spare her death, the creatures of the forest made an incision on another tree, which resulted in its red sap turning into a heart. Ever since, this tree has been called the Blood Tree. The maiden gave birth to twins, Hunahpú and Ixbalanqué, who in time avenged their parents, destroying the evil lords of the underworld. After a life of outstanding achievements and deeds, the twin heroes born from a tree gained their place in the heavens, becoming the sun and the moon.

MORRO OR JÍCARO
(Calabash)

In their opinion, this was a wonderful sort of tree,
because of what happened one time when they put
the head of Hun-Hunahpú between its branches.

And the nobles of Xibalbá decreed:
"No one may pick this fruit!
No one may stand beneath this tree!"
they said,
and thus they ordered to block the way
for all the people of Xibalbá.

The head of Hun-Hunahpú did not appear again,
because it had changed into a fruit
of the tree that is called calabash.
Nevertheless, a girl heard the marvellous story.
Now we will tell you how it came about.

Popol Vuh

Botanical name:

Crescentia cujete L.

Family:

Bignoniaceae

Synonyms:

C. acuminata Kunth

C. angustifolia Willd. ex Seem.

C. arborea Raf.

C. cuneifolia Gardner

C. fasciculata Miers

C. plectantha Miers

C. spatulata Miers

Common names:

Morro, Jícara, Mulul, Jicarero, Xigal (Pipil de Salamá), Hom (Q'eqchi') Huaz, Güiro, Luch, Tecomate (Mayan names). Calabash, Gourd tree.

The Morro (*Crescentia cujete*) in Traditional Lore:

This type of calabash is as much a part of Maya tradition as the apple tree in Judeo-Christian history as told by Genesis. The historical importance of *Crescentia cujete* is manifested in the Popol Vuh, where the tree is mentioned several times.

Just like Eve, Ixquic was tempted, disobeyed, and went to the forbidden tree to pick fruit. As she tried to reach for the magic fruit, she received a spurt of saliva in her hand which made her pregnant. This is how Hunahpú and Ixbalanqué were conceived.

Calabash trees were among the most highly valued plants of the pre-Columbian Meso-American world, whether cultivated or wild.

Bowls called jícaras, or calabash cups, made from the dried fruits have great ethnological significance in Central América and Mexico. They are decorated with colored or black carved designs. Fernández de Oviedo relates that in Panama and Costa Rica, calabashes were coated with gold or adorned with gold handles for use by the native nobility.

In the colonial period, the wood was used for making stirrups, which were also decorated with carvings. The word jícaro, a common name for calabash in Spanish, appears in several place names, such as El Jícaro, a village in El Progreso, and El Jicaral, in Chiquimula. It is believed that the name "Jicaltepeque" means "mountain of calabashes."

The trees provide excellent habitats for epiphytic orchids and bromeliads.

The calabash is native to tropical América, although it has been successfully introduced to warm regions of Europe, Africa and Asia. In Guatemala, it is found in Petén, Alta and Baja Verapaz, Izabal, Santa Rosa, Esquintla, Suchitepéquez, Retalhuleu, San Marcos and El Quiché; nevertheless, it has been declared an endangered species. Nowadays, the calabash tree is used for its medicinal properties, and the fruits serve as raw material for the manufacture of utensils such as bowls, spoons, rattles, money boxes and scales. The artisans of Rabinal, a town in Baja Verapaz, Guatemala, notably the Sis family, are famous for their work with calabashes.

Description:

The tree is 7 to 10 meters tall, with a thick trunk; the crown is round, wide, and open, with few extending branches. The nodes on the branches are bulky. They bear twigs with 3 to 5 simple, spatulate leaves, on short petioles. At the end of the branches the leaves are clustered. The calabash is evergreen. The flowers grow directly on the trunk, or on the thickest branches. They are bell-shaped, 5 to 6 cm long, light yellow or dark green, with dark purple veins. The fruits vary in size (up to 25 cm); they are elongated and egg-shaped, or round. Some varieties of *Crescentia* bear small fruit. The hard, thin hull surrounds a whitish and juicy pulp which contains many small, brown seeds, 0.6 cm long. The wood is white, but as it dries it becomes a very light brown. It is moderately hard and heavy, firm, resistant and elastic.

Ecological Requirements:

The calabash tree grows in humid, semi-humid, as well as semi-arid regions, at elevations of less than 350 meters above sea level. It thrives in many different kinds of soil and does not tolerate low temperatures.

Propagation:

If large seeds are available, these can be planted directly into the field. Calabash trees can also be propagated by making cuttings. In either case, the seedlings, or cuttings, require sufficient maintenance to prevent weeds, etc., from hampering their growth. The young trees grow slowly.

Planting:

As shade trees on pasture grounds, *Crescentia* can be planted 10 meters or more apart. In gardens and along fences, they can be planted as close together as 2 meters.

Main Uses:

Once dry and rid of its inner pulp, the gourdlike fruit has countless practical uses. Calabashes are used as water containers, decorations, musical instruments (maracas, rattles), bowls for collecting rubber, money boxes, and different kinds of utensils. "Jícaras" are bowls obtained by cutting a fruit in two parts. The dry and hollow halves are used for serving hot chocolate and other traditional drinks such as atol (a gruel made out of ground maize cooked with water, salt, sugar and milk), posol, pinolillo (roasted maize flour mixed with water, sugar and cocoa) and boj (oatmeal cooked in water, milk and cinnamon). Calabash bowls are often decorated with designs of plants and animals. The decorations are applied using "nij" (*Llaveia axin,* a type of scale insect) and soot. Ripe fruits are eaten by cattle during the dry season, but there is a belief among herdsmen that this leads to miscarriages. The fleshy part of young fruits is edible - it is used in the preparation of sweets and drinks - and has numerous medicinal properties as well. In particular, the sweetened inner pulp of the calabash is used in the preparation of cough syrup and cold remedies. A poultice of crushed, soft calabash is used for treating skin burns.

Crescentia wood is easy to work and a nice finish can be obtained. When the wood is still green it is easy to carve; once it is dry, it is as hard as iron.

Crescentia cujete. Tree.

41

Botanical name:

Crescentia alata Kunth

Family:

Bignoniaceae

Synonyms:

Parmentiera alata (H.B.K.) Miers

Common names:

Morro, Lajmulul or Simax, Rutc (Ch'orti').
Calabash.

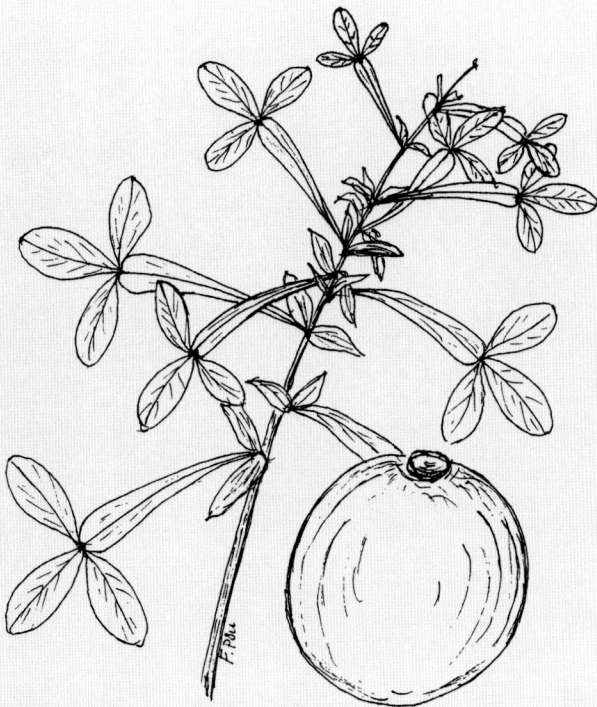

The Morro (*Crescentia alata*) in Traditional Lore:

Another species, *Crescentia alata,* is found in Guatemala in Izabal, Alta and Baja Verapaz, Zacapa, Chiquimula, El Progreso, Jalapa, Jutiapa, Santa Rosa, as well as in Mexico and other parts of Central América. It has been introduced to the Philippines and to other islands in the Pacific. The leaves of this species are shaped like a cross. This characteristic did not go unnoticed by the Spanish conquerors who attributed a supernatural significance to it. Oviedo wrote in a manuscript 400 years ago: "Each leaf has the shape of a cross, and this is very important because it is testimony of the cross, of which these people must have been aware."

Description:

Crescentia alata are small trees, usually not exceeding 12 meters, with a round, spreading crown. The trunk has a diameter of up to 50 cm; the branches are thick, and sometimes entwined. The bark is light brown, and has scales or deep cracks. The leaves are trifoliate and coriacious. The flowers are dark purple, occasionally with light purple stripes. The fruit of *C. alata* is oval or round, and is generally smaller than the fruit of *C. cujete*. In the field, the two species are differentiated by the leaf shape. The leaves of *C. cujete* are simple (not branched), whereas those of *C. alata* are trifoliate, in the shape of a cross.

Ecological Requirements:

Crescentia alata is quite common on dry hillsides and plains, although it sometimes also grows in more humid areas up to 1200 meters above sea level, such as the south coast and the eastern part of Guatemala. It is found in dry, tropical forests and thorn scrub.

Main Uses:

The characteristics and applications of the wood of both types are similar. They are often found on pastures, where they have a dual purpose: to serve as a shade tree and, given the sweet pulp inside the fallen calabashes, as an extra food source of food for livestock.

Crescentia cujete. Fruits: bowls.

Crescentia alata. Artisan working with the fruits.

Crescentia alata. Fruits: drinking cups.

*The forest is present throughout the Popol Vuh;
many other trees are named repeatedly . All
the stories of the work portray clearly and with
literary beauty the primary role of Nature in
Maya beliefs and values. The divine strength
of its heroes comes from this understanding: the
wise use of and respect for the forces of Nature.*

*The Wacah Chan and the Popol Vuh are the
clearest examples of the mysticism given to
trees by the Maya civilization. Many other
manifestations of special significance are still
evident in rituals and ceremonies, with incense
taken from their sap and wood being burnt.*

*Trees are an inseparable part of the cosmic
perspective of the Maya. The importance that
forests have enjoyed throughout their history is
expressed in their most sacred beliefs.*

*Trees are magic because they are useful in
many different ways: trees are mystic because
they have a role, a spirit, a color.
Trees sustain the world. Trees are Life.*

Trees as Nourishment

Due to the diverse ecosystems, the area has an extraordinary variety of trees. The Maya civilization was keenly aware of their myriad properties and, accordingly, took the best from the forests. It is believed that the first inhabitants of Mesoamérica populated the fertile Pacific coast. The Maya civilization flourished centuries later in the northern lowlands of Petén. Still today, the vast jungle of the Petén is lush and plentiful, although large tracts have been cleared by illicit logging operations, and is home to a wide variety of flora and fauna. The ancient Maya respectfully accepted the gifts of their rich surroundings, and they applied many different uses to the vast array of trees which were found in their vicinity.

Trees as Nourishment

Indigenous species provide nourishment through their seeds, leaves and, in the case of palm trees, the core. For food, the ancient Maya cultivated the land and gathered the vast array of jungle produce. The wise and systematic use of these resources was a major factor for their survival and, indeed, for the development and splendor of their culture.

Ramón was a basic part of Maya diet. Evidence suggests that the fruit was used in addition to maize to make "tortillas" when the latter was in short supply. Studies have shown that the organized cultivation of ramón was essential for the subsistence of the Maya civilization. This implies a culture with an advanced concept of forest use and preservation. The ramón was also frequently used in building.

The Kaqchikel, Maya who still inhabit the Guatemalan highlands, called this tree Iximché, or Tree of Maize, and gave the same name to their kingdom. Several ramón trees were found in the surroundings of the ancient city. Since this tree grows only in the lowlands, it is believed that the Kaqchikel imported it and developed a technique for its cultivation. At present, the ramón has many different uses, particularly in agriculture and carpentry. In Petén it is still consumed as food when the maize harvest is scarce.

Many other trees were and are used as food by the Maya. Among them, the zapote, whose fruit remains appreciated throughout Central América; the zapotón, a close relative that grows in the Atlantic wetlands, although not eaten by humans, is excellent nourishment for fish; the avocado, now found in markets around the world in a variety of hybrids; and the nance, or wild cherry, whose sweet fruit is referred to as a very special treat in the Popol Vuh. And then there was cacao, it is believed that the the ancient Maya drank chocolate ground with an hallucinogenic flower in some of their sacred rituals. Cocoa beans were so valued that they were used as currency. After the decline of the Mayan civilization in Petén, the Pacific lowlands saw the rise of the Pipil nation, based primarily on cacao cultivation and commerce. Their monopoly of this precious fruit engaged them in a war against the powerful highland K'iche' and Kaqchikel, who were already fighting against each other. When the Spaniards arrived, they found these kingdoms weakened by war and took strategic advantage to accomplish the "Conquest." Chocolate then became known around the globe; today, Maya continue to drink it during celebrations. In fact, some of the finest quality cacao in the world is grown in this region.

CACAO

*"This will be our food: maize, pepper seeds, beans,
pataxte, cacao: all of this is yours, and if something
is saved or overlooked, it also will be yours, consume
it!" so said Hunahpú and Ixbalanque to the mouse.*

Popul Vuh

Botanical name:

Theobroma cacao L.

Family:

Sterculiaceae

Common names:

Cacao, Cacau.

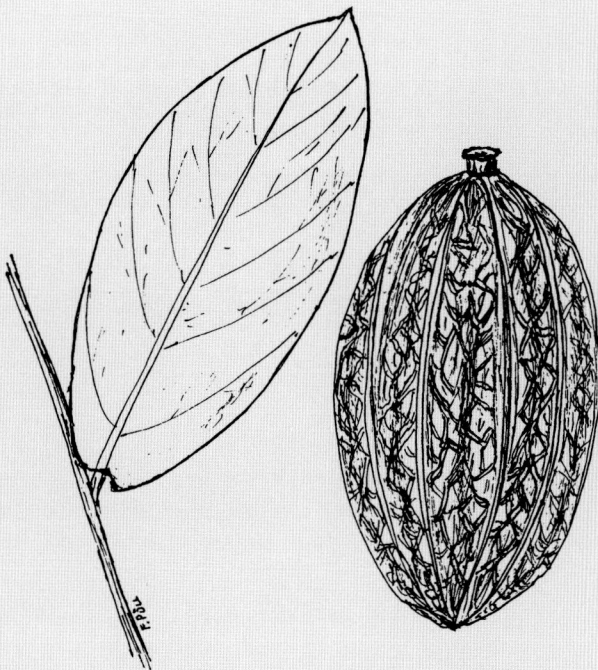

The Cacao in Traditional Lore:

The most frequently mentioned plant in Maya history is the cacao tree. Originally, it produced an incomparable beverage, then was used as currency and later, as a basic ingredient in chocolate-making.

The name cacao comes from the Náhuatl tongue cacahuatl. Aware of its high nutritional value and exquisite flavor, Linnaeus named it *Theobroma*, which in Latin means food of the gods. It was the favorite drink of the Maya elite and is still used in rituals and special celebrations. The Aztecs fed choclatl to their prisoners -"to transform their hearts to chocolate"- and then tear them out and offer them to the gods.

Chocolate can be prepared in several ways and served hot or cold. A cup of chocolate has 600 calories and is high in iron and magnesium. Probably because of this, Hernán Cortés (conqueror of Mexico) praised chocolate saying; "With one cup of chocolate you can walk all day."

The Maya civilization used cacao as currency until the Spanish conquest. The Spanish, charmed by the unique flavor, imported cacao beans to Spain, so when presented by Cortés in 1528, it was widely accepted and called "a drink made for kings." During the colonial era, cacao was the main export product of Guatemala and only later, was it replaced by coffee, indigo and seeds.

Although cacao was native to Mesoamérica, Spain spread it around the world, and Switzerland perfected its refinement.

Description:

The cacao tree is small, 6 to 8 meters tall, with sparse dark brown branches. The elliptical leaves that measure 15 to 30 cm long are thick and have short petioles. The small yellow flowers bloom on the trunk and lower branches. The oval shaped fruit, approximately 20 cm long and 8 cm wide, has

10 furrows. It is filled with a milky-white pulp that protects about 50 flat seeds that are 2 to 2.5 cm long.

The cacao fruit, commonly known as mazorca or pocha, is a stone fruit, sustained by a short wooden stalk that grows from the thicker part of the trunk. Shape and size vary according to each type, and may be elongated, melon or pumpkin-shaped, and the ripe fruit is light yellow to dark red.

Ecological Requirements:

Cacao grows mainly in the Suchitepéquez, Escuintla, and Alta Verapaz departments of Guatemala. It is believed to be originally from tropical América, possibly the upper Amazon area, and has been cultivated for many years in Mexico and Guatemala.

It prospers from 200 to 600 meters above sea level, with a minimum precipitation of 1500 mm spread uniformly over the entire year; it needs a minimum temperature of 21° C and withstands a maximum of 30° C. The cacao tree should be planted in level, or slightly sloping areas. Loose and deep soil is needed and, if possible, virgin soil would be best with a pH of 5.5 to 8.5. The tree should always have shade, and the mother-of-cacao (*Gliricidia sepium*) tree, *Inga* spp. and *Leucaena* spp. are highly recommended for this purpose. Shade trees should be planted spaced 8 x 8 square meters apart within the plantation.

Propagation:

The cacao tree can be propagated in four ways: by seed, grafting, or from cuttings and by shoots. Seeds are mostly used but not highly recommended because of the genetic variability. Seed can be germinated in two ways: directly in its definitive locality, or in a nursery to be transplanted at a future date.

Each cacao fruit contains around 25 to 30 seeds (almonds or nibs), usually found in 5 rows over a central placenta.

Grafting is widely used because the positive aspects of the tree, such as production and disease resistance, are cloned. In Guatemala, the patch graft is the most used.

For reproduction from cuttings, shoots with 4 or 5 leaves are best. They are left in moist growbags for 30 days until they begin to sprout roots, and after 3 months they can be transplanted to their definitive site. However, this method is not widely used because of its high cost and labor requirements.

Planting:

Cacao trees should be planted at a distance of 4 x 4 square meters, in holes 1.5' deep and 1' wide. They may be planted from May until October, although trees planted in October may not prosper.

Main Uses:

Cacao's main use is to make chocolate. Almost all the native lowland population drinks this beverage. The seed, when pressed, produces an oil that is used in cosmetics, perfumes and medicines.

The seeds have up to 53% oil (cacao butter), 14% protein and 7% starch; and contain an alkaloid stimulant (theobromine) similar to caffeine.

Theobroma cacao. Fruits and seeds.

RAMÓN

And thou shalt know that in the heart of the wild jungle
whence the tranquility of the tree is alive,
whence the shout of the irate wild beast was born
and the bird with sweet tenderness nested,
there was man's first crib,
there the spoken expression sprang from his lips
and he became the master of all created things!

But man, ungrateful of his mother jungle,
of his brother, the tree,
soon forgot when he formed a nation.
Today his mind ignores
that the jungle also speaks to the gods
and his brother tree has voice that can sing!

When the Chirimia and the Tun Were Born
José Luis García A.

Botanical name:

Brosimum alicastrum Swartz

Family:

Moraceae

Synonyms:

Brosimum latifolium Standl.

Common names:

Ramón, Confitura, Iximché, Leche María, Masico, Masiquilla, Mojo, Mujú, Muñeco, Nazareno, Ojite, Ojoche, Ox, Ujo, Ujushte blanco, Nuez de pan, Ajah, Tsotz-ax, Ax, Mo, Talcoite.
Bread Nut.

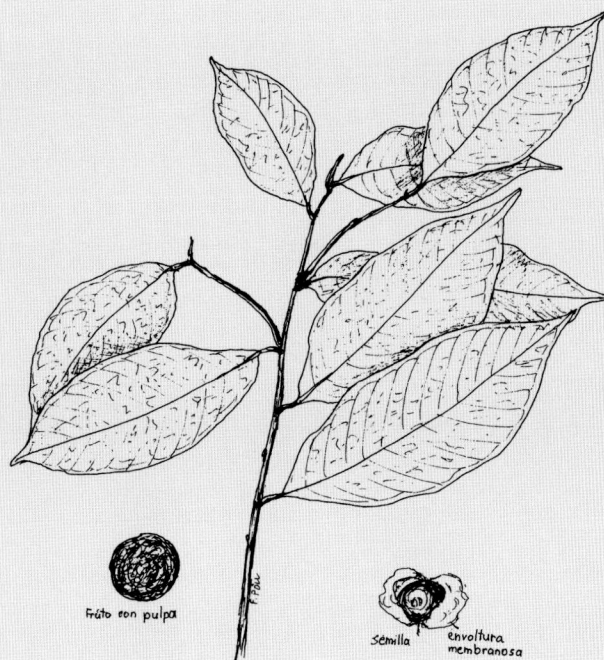

Frúto con pulpa

Sémilla   envoltura membranosa

The Ramón in Traditional Lore:

The Maya, who constructed and maintained a large quantity of buildings and ceremonial centers, constantly had large work groups. The Pulestons in their report on the ramón tree*, indicated that production of this kind of tree allowed for more time and energy to be devoted to other agricultural chores, especially to the clearing of land to plant maize. This and other reasons prompted them to develop the following theory: The Classic Maya intensely developed the ramón tree, and probably other agricultural products, in their residential areas. Maize, although it was a desirable food source, may have played a lesser role in Maya diet than previously thought. The Maya people were creative and hard-working, well adjusted to life in the jungle because of their intelligent use of the natural resources. Not only the Maya took advantage of the ramón tree; the ancient Kaqchikel, who named it the "Iximché", did so as well. In their dialect Ixim means corn and chée means tree. They held this tree in such high esteem that they named their most important city after it. It should also be noted that, although not common to the region, the ramón tree was found in areas around the Iximché ruins, located in a humid mountainous region. This leads us to believe that they were specifically planted as food or for ceremonial purposes.

Description:

The ramón tree can reach up to 40 meters in height, and its trunk can measure up to 1 meter in diameter. It is subperrenifolious, that is, it sheds some of its leaves at a certain time of year. The trunk is cylindrical and grooved, and its butressed roots help sustain the tree. The sap is milky, the bark smooth and light gray; and the core hard wood is bright red, while the outer layers are yellowish.

*Presented in the Thirty-third Assembly of the American Society of Archeology: "The Ramón: The Base of the Nutritive Diet of the Ancient Mayas of Tikal D.E. Puleston, P.O. Puleston. USA: 1986."

The crown foliage is dense, made up of long, thick and shiny leaves. The orange colored fruit is round, the seed is rich in starches, and is odorless and flavorless. The ramón flourishes in the Pacific coastal area and in the Guatemalan northwest and is a favorite food for forest animals.

Ecological Requirements:

The ramón grows in hot, humid tropical forests. It requires between 2100 and 4300 mm of annual rainfall, temperatures between 21° and 25° C, and an altitudinal range of 80 to 1600 meters above sea level.

It can adapt to various climates, ranging from semi-humid to semi-arid and can flourish even in poor or moderately fertile soils that are shallow or poorly drained, with textures ranging from clayey to sandy, although the ramón does prefer rocky, limestone hills.

Propagation:

This tree reproduces by seeds that quickly lose their germinative power. In the shade under ramón trees in Tikal National Park, dense seedling populations with 1300 to 2400 per square meter are found, and these seedlings can be transplanted to other areas.

Planting:

In Mexico, the ramón tree is planted at a distance of 4 to 6 meters apart. In areas of intense cultivation, they may be planted in rows 1.55 or 2 meters apart, with 24 or 30 centimeters between plants.

Production:

A ramón tree annually produces 50 to 75 kilos of fruit; and food for a whole family for a year could be provided by harvesting about 1360 kilos. Trees can be pruned two or three times a year, and the foliage used as fodder, each harvest producing about 10 to 15 tons of leaves per hectare.

In the lowest density areas, each ramón tree can produce about 4.3 liters of latex, and a minimum of 5.11 cubic meters of lumber.

Main Uses:

This is a multi-use tree. Its leaves, stems and seeds are used as cattle fodder, especially during drought. The leaves increase milk production in cattle. The seeds are rich in protein, amino acids, iron and vitamin C; they can be cooked, ground into flour, or roasted to prepare a drink similar to chocolate. Although the wood is used in construction, it is appreciated more for fine furniture, carved items, flooring, saddles and bowls. It is also used in the manufacture of sports equipment. Its pulp is used for paper.

A special latex used to prepare a non-dairy milk can be processed from the bark, and ramón trees can also be planted as decorative hedges and wind-breaks, and as shade trees, especially in coffee plantations.

Although the ramón was one of the basic foods of the ancient Maya, today its use as food is rare. In some areas of Petén, however, it is consumed when the maize harvest is poor.

Brosimum alicastrum. Fruits.

ZAPOTE

This fruit too is very abundant and there are many different varieties. Some are very red, others whitish. Others very dark and called "mulattos." Others are grafted, of which we have seen at least eight different types throughout the area. Others are called black zapotes and their flesh is similar to the fruit of drumstick tree.

The Natural History of the Kingdom of Guatemala
Fray Francisco Ximenez

Botanical name:

Pouteria sapota (Jacq.) H.E. Moore & Stearn

Family:

Sapotaceae

Synonyms:

Achradelpha mammosa (L.) O.F. Cook
Achras mammosa L.
Calocarpum mammosum (L.) Pierre
Calocarpum sapota (Jacq.) Merr.
Lucuma mammosa (L.) Gaertn.
Pouteria mammosa (L.) Cronquist
Sideroxylon sapota Jacq.

Common names:

Zapote, Satul, Sesatul (Q'eqchi'), Tulul (Kaqchikel), Saltul (Poqomchi'), Zapote Mamey (México), Chacalhaas (Yucatán Maya), Mamey, Mamey Colorado (Yucatán).
Marmalade Plum.

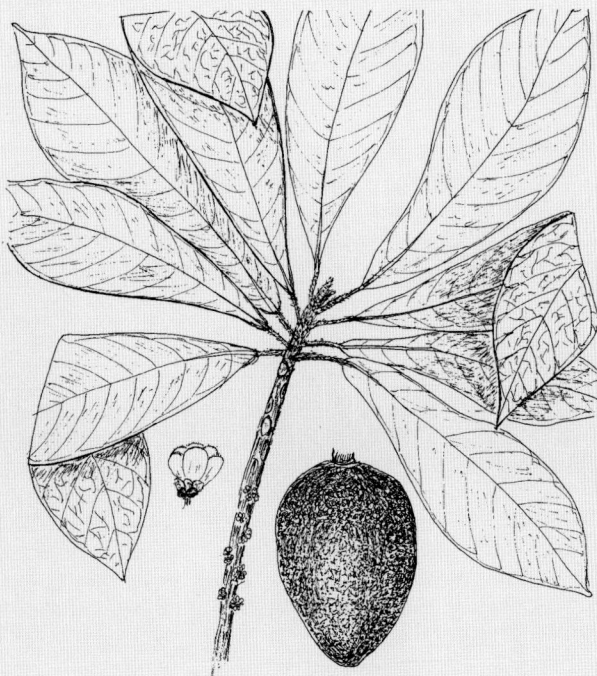

The Zapote in Traditional Lore:

The zapote fruit is widely consumed in Central América, not only by humans but also by animals. Its wood is almost never used.

As the legend goes, Hernán Cortes' soldiers ate zapote fruit all along their march towards Honduras in 1524.

The name zapote comes from the Aztec word "tzapotl," a generic term that groups together several species of large, sweet spherical fruits.

Even when country laborers were clearing the jungle, they always left zapote trees intact. These are frequently found on land that has been used exclusively for cultivating corn. Enormous ancient trees can be found in the Pacific littoral and in hilly areas.

Description:

The zapote tree is very leafy, and can grow up to 30 meters tall. Its trunk is cylindrical and straight, wider at its base, and can measure up to 1.5 meters in diameter. The bark is brown and rough. The crown is very large, with a regular amount of thick branches that extend their dense foliage over a large radius. The leaves are from 15 to 30 cm long, oval or lanceolate, and are grouped together at the end of the newest branches.

The flowers are large, 6 to 10 mm in diameter, in short peduncles at the leaf axis or in leafless groups. The zapote fruit can be round or oval and has a tough, irregular reddish-brown rind. The flesh is red, orange or grayish, very juicy and smooth, and when ripe, is aromatic, soft and very sweet. It contains one or two ellipsoidal pointed and shiny smooth black seeds, from 5 to 6 cm long.

Ecological Requirements:

The zapote tree requires a tropical climate; it prospers at altitudes of less than 600 meters but can flourish at up to 1400 meters above sea level. The climate should be humid (from 1500 to 3000 mm annual rainfall). At drought-free sites, fruit can be harvested year round. The tree reproduces better in a climate with average temperatures of 25° to 28° C. It cannot withstand low temperatures (less than 15°C), not even for short periods. It adapts well to acid or clayey soil that is deep, fertile and well drained; it will not prosper in swampy, rocky or limey soil.

The zapote is native to Central América (the Izabal and Petén departments in Guatemala) and is very common in Mexico.

Propagation:

The zapote reproduces by untreated seeds. The seeds can be stored, but this is not advisable as the fruit-bearing period is delayed and the characteristics of some varieties may be lost.

Breaking the shell of the seed can accelerate germination. The seeds should be planted in large bags or beds, in loose soil previously disinfected with fungicides, and laid horizontally 5 cm apart in shallow soil. They will germinate in a month. Weaker plantlets should be eliminated because they take too long to grow. When 20 to 25 cm tall, the plants should be transplanted to growbags to develop in a nursery for 5 months and then planted at their definitive site. If reproduced by grafting, the productive characteristics will be improved and the period between planting and harvest will be reduced by half. Grafting is used to accelerate production, but this process has to be carried out swiftly, otherwise, latex, a milky sap, will soon cover the wound. One week after grafting, the apex of the stock should be cut, allowing 30 cm between the bud and the graft area; this should be repeated after 15 days, eliminating all but the grafted area. After 2 months the bud will begin to sprout and after 4 months, the tape should be removed thus allowing the new sprout to grow freely. The new plants can be transplanted 2 months later to their definitive site.

The different zapote varieties are obvious and based on size and shape, and they can weigh from 1 to 6 pounds.

Main Uses:

The sweet and aromatic zapote fruit is consumed fresh in milkshakes, ice cream and candy, and is cooked for use in jams and confectionery. In Guatemala, zapote is used to make very popular native candies.

The seed, roasted and mixed with cacao, is used to make chocolate to which it contributes a bitter taste and characteristic fragrance. Zapote fruit is rich in vitamin A and C, carbohydrates, calcium and phosphorus and is said to have medicinal properties.

Zapote wood, dark or shiny red or ochre, is consistent and strong, long lasting and heavy. It is used in fine furniture, cabinets, pillars, decorative beams, handicrafts, tool handles, carvings and stands. It is not resistant to humidity and will rot easily. It is moderately resistant to fungus and insects.

The seeds are called 'sapuyules' or 'sapuyulos' and can be found sun dried hanging from twine or sticks in the marketplaces all year round. Ground, they add flavor to gruel and other beverages as well as to chocolate. Because of its natural oil, the stone is used to make soap and special hair oils that produce a natural shine and softness. In some places, zapote oil is thought to prevent hair loss and to stimulate hair growth.

Pouteria sapota. Mature fruit with seed.

ZAPOTÓN

For nine miles the passage continued thus one scene of unvarying beauty, when suddenly the narrow river expanded into a large lake, encompassed by mountains and studded with islands, which the setting sun illuminated with gorgeous splendor. We remained on deck till a late hour, and awoke the next morning in the harbour of Yzabal.

Incidents of Travel in Central América, Chiapas and Yucatán

John L. Stephens, 1842

Botanical name:

Pachira aquatica Aubl.

Family:

Bombacaceae

Synonyms:

Bombax aquaticum (Aubl.) K. Schum.

B. macrocarpum (Schltdl. & Cham.) K. Schum.

B. rigidifolium Ducke

C. macrocapa Schltdl. & Cham.

Carolinea princeps L.f.

Pachira macrocarpa (Schltdl. & Cham.) Walp.

Other species:

Pachira longiflora (Mart & Zucc.) Decne.

Common names:

Zapotón, Zapote bobo, Pumpumjunche, Uacoot (Petén, Maya).

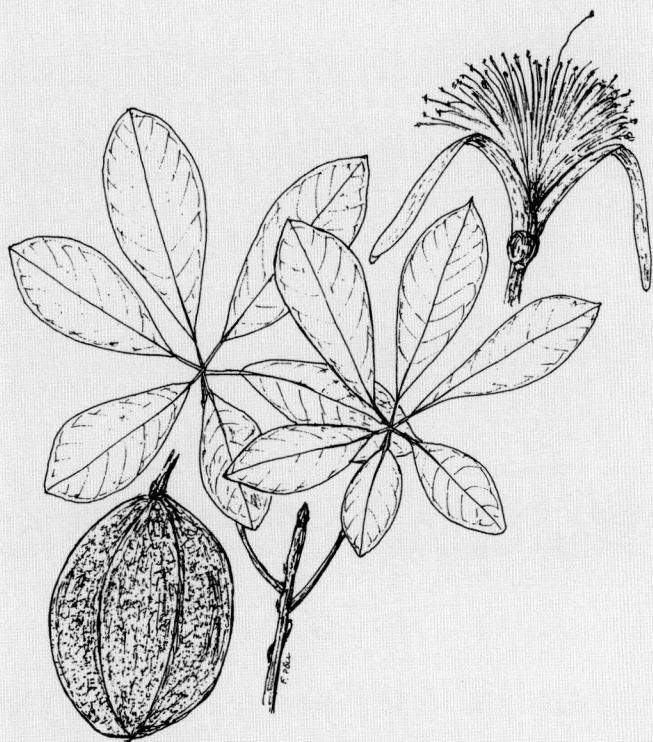

The Zapotón in Traditional Lore:

This tree is commonly found in thickets in shallow open swamplands. On the shores of the Río Dulce and Izabal lake in Guatemala, the zapotón grows side-by-side with mangroves and is very important in preventing erosion; the long roots sustain the earth and prevent its being washed away by water currents. It is astounding how this tree can support its many large and abundant fruits. Because of the beauty of its blossom and shape of its branches, it is also used as a shade and ornamental tree.

Description:

The zapotón tree is 15 to 20 meters high. Its short trunk ranges from 25 to 60 cm in diameter, and in some instances can be arched and crooked. It has aerial roots that are generally long and slender to ease support; the bark is thick and bland, light tan or gray, slightly cracked; and the roots are sparse and close to the surface. The alternate leaves have five to eight leaflets, are quite thick and have a long petiole.

The blossoms are large and colorful due to the long reddish-purple filaments of the stamens. The narrow petals are up to 30 cm long, covered by yellowish hairs on the outside and white ones on the inside.

The dark brown fruit is a large capsule, oblong-ellipsoidal in shape, 20 to 30 cm long and 10 to 12 cm in diameter, weighing from 1000 to 1500 grams. Each tree produces approximately 50 to 80 fruits a year, and each capsule contains 25 seeds, which are irregular in shape and about 3 cm in diameter.

The main habitat of the zapotón is along both the Atlantic and the Pacific coastlines. The highest altitude in which it can be found is around San Felipe Retalhuleu and near the lakes and streams. Zapotón can be found in the departments of Izabal, Santa Rosa, Escuintla, Suchitepéquez, San Marcos and Petén; and in southern areas of Mexico, Belize, Panama and South América.

Ecological Requirements:

This tree grows naturally on the shorelines of streams and lakes, close to mangroves and in areas frequently flooded by fresh water. It grows best in sandy or sandy-clay soils, withstanding a wide temperature range and the natural humidity of the tropics. It grows well up to about 300 meters above sea level.

Propagation:

The zapotón reproduces by seed or by cuttings; in the countryside it usually spreads naturally. The seeds frequently disperse via waterways, need no preparative treatment, and germinate in 8 to 10 days. They are collected from May to July. The zapotón can be reproduced through cuttings when the trees are 2 to 8 inches in diameter, and 2 to 4 meters long. This system has been very successful if cuttings planted at the beginning of the rainy season. Initially, growth is quite rapid. These plants can measure up to 60 cm tall two weeks after germination. The first flowering occurs after 4 or 5 years.

Main Uses:

The zapotón is best known as an ornamental, and in Guatemala is little used as a food. A white, odorless good quality oil can be extracted from the seeds and used for industrial purposes. On the Atlantic coast of Nicaragua, however, the seeds are cooked and eaten. Known as saba nuts, they have a taste similar to chestnuts (*Castanea sativa*). In certain regions of Mexico, the seeds are roasted and eaten as a side dish; when ripe they can be chopped and fried in oil, or simply boiled with salt. The seeds that have fallen off the trees into the water are avidly devoured by fish and turtles. In some areas of South América, the new leaves are also eaten.

The bark can be used to caulk ships and make ropes; it releases a dark red dye that is used to dye sails, rope and fishing gear.

The soft white wood is used to make paper, boxes and crates, toys, plywood and other objects.

Pachira aquatica. Flower with frog.

NANCE
(Wild cherry)

This is the great tree of Seven Macaw, a nance,
and this is the food of Seven Macaw. In order
to eat the fruit of the nance he goes up the tree
everyday. Since Hunaphu and Xbalanque have
seen where he feeds, they are now hiding beneath
the tree of Seven Macaw, they are keeping quiet
here, the two boys are in the leaves of the tree.

Popul Vuh

Botanical name:

Byrsonima crassifolia (L.) Kunth

Family:

Malpighiaceae

Synonyms:

Byrsonima cotinifolia Kunth

B. karwinskiana Juss.

B. laurifolia var. *guatemalensis* Nied.

B. pulchra DC.

B. rufescens Bertol.

Malphighia crassifolia L.

Common names:

Nance Dulce, Chitapal, Chi (K'ekchí), Tapal (Kaqchikel, Poqomchí), Craboo (Belize), Xacpán (Maya Yucatán), Nanchi (Oaxaca, Veracruz), Crabao (Honduras), Murici, Murici-do-pria (Brazil), Maricas, Simarrón (Cuba), Chaparro Manteca, Sebanero (Venezuela), Nanciato (Honduras), Nacé (Panama), Nancité (El Salvador), Yuco, Naci Chaparro (Colombia), Quinaquina des savanes (French Guiana).

Wild cherry.

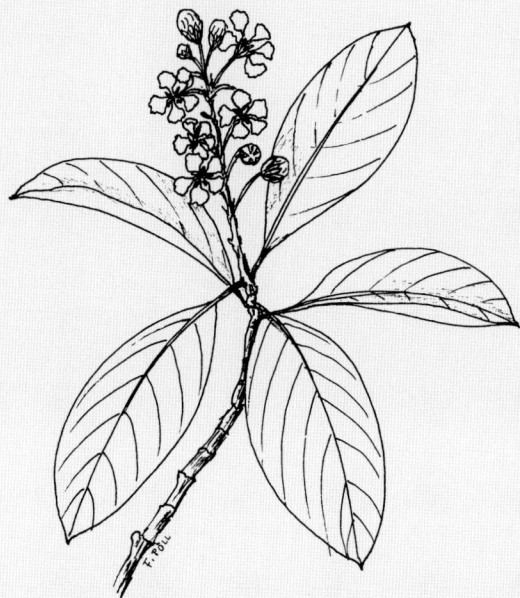

The Nance in Traditional Lore:

Before the discovery of América, the local natives were well acquainted with the fruit of the nance, or wild cherry, and it is mentioned in the Popul Vuh.

The name 'nance' originated from the Náhuatl language used in all Central América, and has given rise to terms such as El Nanzal, the nance plantation.

Nance fruit is very popular in Guatemala. The edible flesh comprises 40% of the fruit, which has a characteristic fragrance and delicious tart taste that takes time to acquire. The fruit may be eaten fresh or preserved, or fermented into a smooth liquor.

Description:

The nance tree can grow 2 to 10 m high. The trunk is twisted and knotted, and often grows horizontally. The bark is cracked with lentil shaped markings; the crown is full of branches that can sweep down to the ground. The opposing leaves are oval, with a shiny green upper surface and with brown hairs on the underside.

Inflorescences flower at the end of the branches and measure up to 12 cm long; the numerous flowers have yellow petals that change to a dark opaque red. The nance fruit is a small round depressed stone fruit about 1.5 to 2 cm in diameter; its yellow skin is very delicate and when ripe the flesh is very juicy, only 5 mm thick, yellow and with characteristic taste and fragance. The seed is round or sometimes pointed, and rarely, two or three may be found in the same fruit.

The nance is found in Mexico, Central América, the Antilles and northern South América, Minas Gerais and Mato Grosso in southern Brazil, Bolivia, Peru, Colombia and the Guyanas.

Ecological Requirements:

The nance grows naturally in open fields, in secondary vegetation and on coastal dunes.

It grows better in sandy soils, but can adapt to any well drained soil.

It prospers in areas that have an annual precipitation over 2000 mm, or if planted near large bodies of water. The mean annual temperature in its ideal habitat is over 20° C. The tree can be found at altitudes from near sea level to 300 to 400 meters.

Propagation:

The nance usually reproduces by seeds that have been discarded after consuming the fruit.

The black, round and hard seeds measure up to 2 cm in diameter and can be stored for several months. They are collected from June to July.

The seeds must be treated before germination; they should be soaked for two days before planting and then placed in beds at a depth of 2 cm. They will germinate after 30 to 40 days; and if planted as soon as possible after extraction from the fruit, they will prosper. When 5 cm tall, they are planted in growbags. If the soil is good, they can be transplanted to their definitive site after 100 to 120 days in the nursery and growth will be rapid.

The seeds can be planted sparsely in beds and then transplanted directly to their definitive site. The ideal plantation should have trees 6 m apart, but the trees can be planted in family gardens. The nance will respond faster if organic compost is placed in its hole.

Grafting has provided positive results. The tree should be pruned to eliminate low branches and form a crown with 6 to 8 main branches. The nance responds well to organic fertilization.

Production:

Blooming, even fruit bearing, can occur early, frequently after the first season, after a year and a half in the field. The fruit can be harvested directly from the tree or off the ground. It should be collected while green for transportation and storage convenience.

When displayed in the market, nance fruits are usually placed in a bowl filled with water, thus preserving them for several days. If placed in a dark container filled with a sugar solution, they will last intact for over 40 days.

The maximum production of a tree after 4 years is from 35 to 40 pounds; the harvest lasts from 4 to 6 months.

Main Uses:

The main product of the nance tree is its fruit. Its lumber is hard and flexible, and is used to make charcoal and firewood. It is also used in rural constructions, furniture and cabinets, wheel spokes for carts, carved instruments and farming tools, as well as for flooring, door and window frames, picture frames and structural beams. The bark is rich in tannin that is used to cure leather, and it also produces a light brown dye effective in coloring cotton material. If the bark is brewed, an astringent home remedy for diarrhea is produced.

Given the beauty of its foliage, flowers and fruit, the nance is used as a shade tree along streets and in parks, churchyards and gardens.

It is widely believed that the concentrated infusion of the bark will cure snakebites and lung problems.

Agriculture is at present a threat to the forest. The ancient Maya succeeded in supporting large populations through adequate land use in conjuction with a balanced relationship with the jungle. Present day inhabitants of the jungle also need to find a balance with the environment. The respect and understanding of the ancient Maya for trees as a foodsource and land protection, is a lesson to be relearned, applied and enjoyed.

Trees Used in Building and Carpentry

The ancient Maya were skilled artists, architects and artisans. They built majestic palaces and colossal pyramids. They produced elaborate potery and refined art, painted outstanding frescoes, and carved exquisitely in both stone and wood.

Trees Used in Building and Carpentry

The majestic mahogany was as precious to the Maya as it was later to the the rest of the world. Unfortunately, the demand for this treasured wood is a major cause of current depredation. Huge areas of Petén have been deforested, mostly through illicit logging and trading operations. Petén's lushness depends totally on the jungle's organic matter, or compost; below, there is only infertile limestone. When the jungle is cleared, the land soon becomes arid and unproductive. It is urgently necessary to control the trade of this precious wood and turn it into an effective, sustainable resource. For its red elegance, mahogany is used mainly in furniture manufacture. The ancients probably used it for similar purposes. However, they knew that besides its beauty, mahogany had medicinal properties: its seeds and bark were used to treat nervous disorders and fevers.

Also highly valued by the Maya was the Spanish cedar, known to them as "the Wood of the Gods." Cedar has a delicate fragance and it too is used in medicine to alleviate bronchitis and epilepsy, among other diseases; however it is used mainly to make furniture. After the arrival of the Spaniards, so many images of Catholic saints were sculpted with cedar wood that this became a tradition. The dramatic change in religion became linguistically evident: the Maya-K'iche' now call cedar "the Wood of the Saints."

"Tzicozapotl" means "Gum Zapote," from which chewing gum was originally obtained. The wood of the chicozapote is extremely durable and was frequently used in Maya constructions for its strength and resistance. An existing - and beautifully carved - lintel from a temple at Tikal (one of the largest Maya ceremonial metropolises) is sixteen hundred years old. The ancient Maya, like others later, chewed on the sap.

Several different species of Guano palm are found in both the northern and southern lowlands. Modern Maya use guano leaves to manufacture hats, fans, brooms, mats, and many other handicrafts, and it is still used to thatch their homes.

Corozo is another type of palm employed in rural constructions in the lowlands of Guatemala. Its leaves, like those of guano, are dried under the strong tropical sun and then carefully plaited to form thatched roofs. It has traditionally been used by the Q'eqchi' people as a cover against the rain, but this use is disappearing due to the use of plastic.

The mangrove is native to both coasts and has traditionally been used by local inhabitants to construct their homes since it is extremely resistant to tough weather conditions and to insects. The submerged mangrove roots create a fertile home for many marine species and with their tangled strength they protect the shores from erosion.

MATILISGUATE

The strongest trees of other lost worlds
will never be as fertile as those here.
If you do not believe that, just gaze upon the Ceiba
and the Matilisguate, who, beat their tousled heads
against the wind, with undecipherable madness
and frenzy.

If a tree is beautiful, it is much more
so if God has given it to us
on our native soil...

To My Country
Roberto Peña

Botanical name:

Tabebuia rosea (Bertol.) A. DC.

Family:

Bignoniaceae

Synonyms:

Couralia rosea (Bertol.) Donn.Sm.

Tabebuia pentaphylla (L). Hemsl.

Tecoma evenia Donn.Sm.

Tecoma punctatissima Kraenzl.

Tecoma rosea Bertol.

Sparattosperma roseum (Bertol.) Miers.

Common names:

Matilisguate, Maqueliz, Matilishuate, Mano de León, Macuelizo, Macueliz, Fresno, Amapola, Amapa, Palo de Rosa, Rosa Morada.

Pink Puoi.

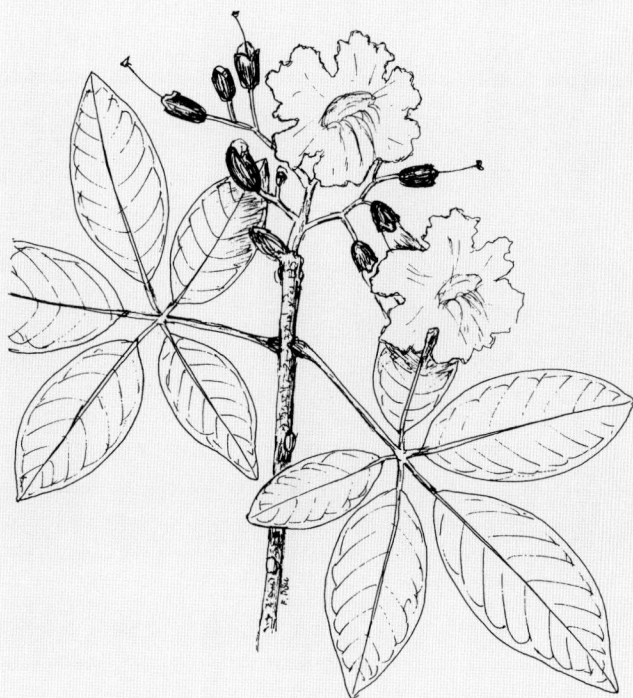

The Matilisguate in Traditional Lore:

The Matilisguate is quite ornamental because of its beautiful flowers. They produce nectar, and an infusion of its leaves can reduce fevers. It is also used as a shade tree in cacao plantations.

Description:

The matilisguate, or pink poui, is a medium sized tree whose trunk can reach 30 meters tall and 70 cm in diameter. The trunk is straight and the crown is sparse. The grayish bark is rough, and the wood is yellowish with several purple patches, fine grained, medium textured, very strong and durable. The branches show scars where many leaves have fallen. The leaves are smooth and thick, and can be stiff; each one is divided into 5 leaflets, like a hand. The flowers are a beautiful sight and may be pink or white. Fruits are found inside long pods and have numerous winged seeds.

Ecological Requirements:

The matilisguate grows at low altitudes, from sea level up to 1000 meters, and in humid climates with 1250 to 2500 mm annual rainfall. It can adapt to dry climates, and prosper in acid or limestone soils, or those that are regularly flooded and constantly muddy.

Propagation:

This tree can be propagated by cuttings or by seed. The seeds may be kept for up to 6 months at room temperature. At a controlled cold temperature, the seeds may last up to 2 years. To plant them, they should be soaked in cold water and sown in seed beds. They will sprout within 12 to 20 days. They should be transplanted to growbags and taken to their final planting destination when the plant is between 25 and 40 cm high.

Planting:

These trees should be planted from 2 to 3 meters apart and must be tended for 3 years. It is very important to maintain the surrounding area weed free.

Production:

During the first year this tree may grow up to 3 meters tall. The plantation should be thinned out after 3 years.

Main Uses:

This wood is widely appreciated because of the variety of uses it offers. You can find Matilisguate wood in informal constructions, fine furniture, paneling, tool handles and handicrafts.

Tabebuia rosea. Flowers.

PALO BLANCO
(Yellow Puoi)

This is the tree song of nature
And hope for the brave country folk,
This is the fragrance of ripening fruits
And the shade that is sought by the wayside.

This is the tree song of springtime,
That perfumes all places around,
While the stream sings along its green edges
And offers the scent of a flower.

To the Tree
Hugo William Avila

Botanical name:

Roseodendron donnell-smithii (Rose) Miranda

Family:

Bignoniaceae

Synonyms:

Cybistax donnell-smithii (Rose) Seibert

Tabebuia donnell-smithii Rose

Common names:

Palo Blanco, Primavera, Duranza, Flor de Zope, San Juan, Cortez, Copal.

Yellow Puoi, Spring bells, Sunshine tree.

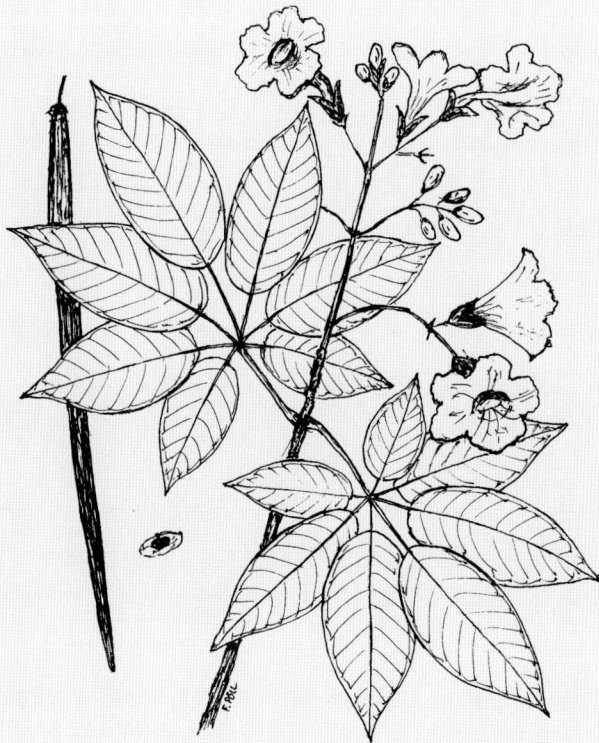

The Palo Blanco in Traditional Lore:

This wood, whether yellowish or white, is very highly valued, and is also called white mahogany. When blooming, the tree's beautiful yellow flowers are very attractive. During World War I, yellow puoi, or palo blanco (white wood) was exported to make airplane propellers.

Description:

The tree is 20 to 30 meters tall. Its trunk can be up to a meter in diameter and its bark is relatively smooth and whitish. The leaves are made up of 5 to 7 smaller leaflets, with very long petioles that can be up to 25 cm long. The flowers bloom in large inflorescences and are a bright strong yellow. The fruits are long pods.

The yellow puoi can be found from southern Mexico through Guatemala to Honduras.

Ecological Requirements:

This tree needs a humid or semi-humid tropical climate, with temperatures between 21° and 25° C, and annual rainfall of 1587 to 4000 mm. It also requires fertile and well-drained soil.

Propagation:

These trees reproduce via seeds that travel by air or are planted in treated areas. Germination begins 12 to 18 days after planting. They should be transplanted when the seedlings are from 2.5 to 5 cm tall, with two opened leaves.

Planting:

Seeds should be planted in growbags; if planted by pseudo-cuttings, these should be at least one meter high, allowing for a stem of 10 to 15 cm.

Production:

The tree grows rapidly and has a 35 year life span.

Main Uses:

This wood has a fine grain and medium texture; it is compact, slightly heavy and resistant. Whether the wood be yellowish or white, it is considered a fine wood although it is not very resistant to humidity. It is widely used in furniture, wood carvings and interior construction. It is a very decorative tree and is used for shade.

Roseodendron donnell-smithii. Flowers.

CAOBA

(Mahogany)

The other great fact of Maya life was the magnificent rain forest, full of towering, liana-draped hardwoods, such as the mahogany, chicozapote, and the most sacred tree of all, the great ceiba. The forest supports a rich web of life, but because the soil under it is thin, nutrients that seep below the surface are captured by the subsoil, which locks them away from the plant roots. The forest has adapted to this by developing a spectacular factory of insects and fungi which live on its dank and shady floor and digest the fall of leaves, limbs, and trees, returning these precious nutrients to the great spreading roots of the trees. This cycle of life is in full view of humanity, a litany of green blossoming out of death and decay.

A Forest of Kings
Linda Schele and David Freidel

Botanical name:

Swietenia macrophylla King

Family:

Meliaceae

Synonyms:

Swietenia belizensis Lundell

Common names:

Caoba, Caoba del Atlántico, Cáguano, Chiculte, Chacalte, Aguano, Punab.
Mahogany.

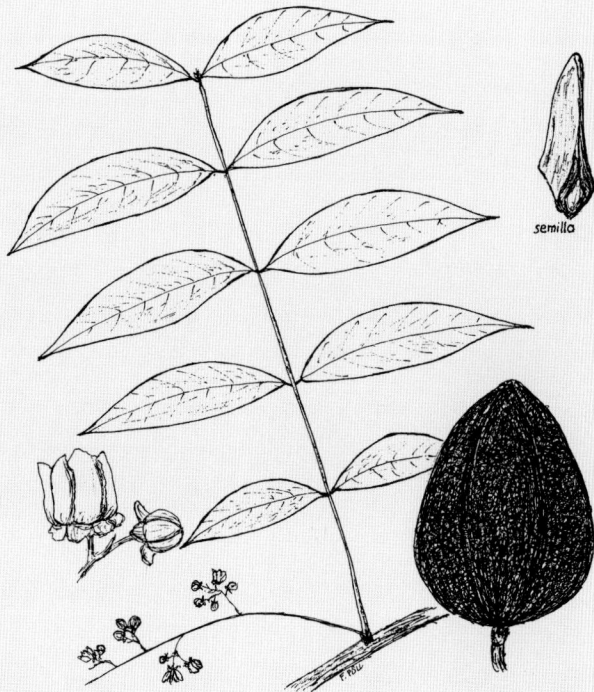

semilla

The Caoba in Traditional Lore:

The caoba (mahogany) and palo campeche (logwood) trees have been very significant in the history of Central América. The colony of Belize was founded to exploit them both. In the seventeenth century, English colonists established settlements and had a prosperous lumber industry. Enormous amounts of mahogany have been exported from Belize, much of which originated in Guatemala, and today it is Belize's national tree.

Description:

The mahogany tree can grow up to 50 meters high. Its trunk is very straight and branchless up to 20 meters, and can have a diameter of 150 cm. The outer bark is dark red, with deep fissures and strong color streaks that turn into a pinkish brown deeper into the tree. It has prominent buttresses (outer roots) which can be up to 4.5 meters long, and form the base of the tree. The crown is very dense, with alternate leaves, compound of 8 to 12 bright green leaflets, 8 to 20 cm long. The flowers bloom in small clusters, and the petals are white and oval shaped. Its fruit is a pear shaped capsule about 12 cm long, that contains reddish-brown winged seeds. This durable wood can range in color from red to salmon, pink or yellow. This tree grows along the entire Atlantic coast, from Mexico to Panama, and in the Amazon region of Peru, Bolivia and Brazil. It has been listed as an endangered species because of unsustainable harvesting.

Ecological Requirements:

Mahogany is native to rain forests and requires from 1000 to 2500 mm of rain annually. It cannot withstand prolonged drought. It may be cultivated in altitudes of over 500 meters, but will not survive frost. It should be planted in loose, deep soil with sufficient drainage, preferably in valley areas, and it will prosper in the shade of taller trees.

Propagation:

These trees reproduce by seeds that are produced in the months of March and April, and are viable up to 4 months at normal temperatures; and from 6 to 12 months in a cold controlled environment. The seeds take around three weeks to sprout and need no previous treatment. During the first 2 months, the seedlings should be kept in a shaded and humid place, and then be transplanted to their final destination at 3 months.

Planting:

Trees should be spaced of 3 or 4 meters apart, with at least 3 to 7 meters between each row. The seedlings grown in bags should be transplanted when they are at least 50 cm high. In case the seedlings are not grown in bags, they have to be 1.50 meters in height for transplantation.

Production:

The mahogany is a fast growing tree. During the first seven years, under favorable circumstances, the tree can grow up to 15 meters. It reaches maturity and in plantations is harvested when it is 35 years old, after having been thinned every 7 years.

Diseases and Pests:

The most dangerous insect is *Hypsiphylla grandella*, a moth which attacks the terminal sprouts of young trees. In areas where these moths occur, interplanting with other species is recommended. Wood-boring insects have also affected this tree, as have fungal diseases.

Main Uses:

The most important product of the mahogany tree is its wood, which is easy to work, of fine quality and exceptional durability. It is renowned as the finest wood for carving, manufacture of fine furniture, sculptures, scientific and musical instruments (especially pianos), ship cabins, carved doors, flooring, household articles and pencils. Seeds and bark provide home remedies that can lower high fevers and ease diarrhea and nervous disorders.

Swietenia macrophylla. Fruits.

CEDRO
(Spanish Cedar)

In the Bible, its history,
In América, its inheritance.
Cedar, native in essence
And glory.

Hai Kais
El Cedro
Flavio Herrera

Botanical name:

Cedrela odorata L.

Family:

Meliaceae

Synonyms:

Cedrela mexicana M. Roem.

Cedrela sintenisii C. DC.

Cedrela yucatana Blake

Common names:

Cedro, Cedro Rojo, Cedro Real, Cedro Oloroso, Cedro del País, Cedro Hembra, Cedro Macho, Culche, Cuche, Yoxcha, Tioxché, Cedro Blanco, Clavel. Spanish Cedar.

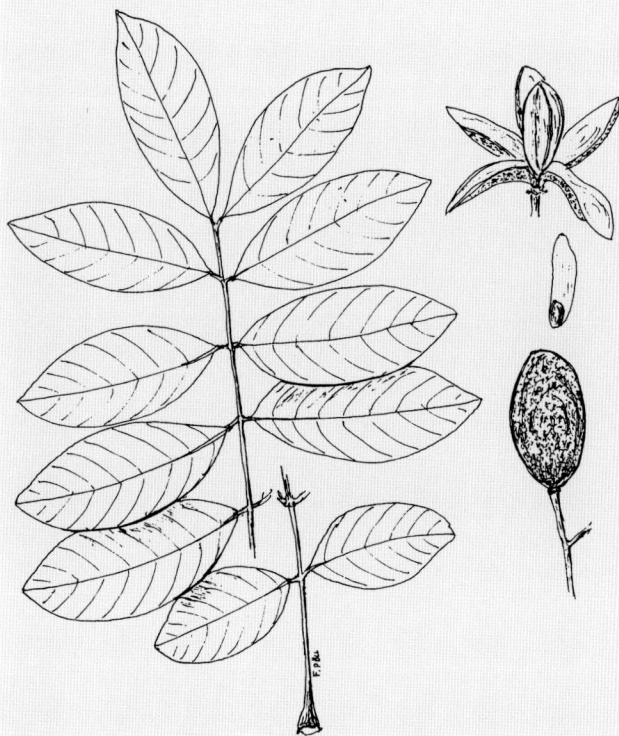

The Cedro in Traditional Lore:

Second only to mahogany, cedar is an important forest product of Guatemala. During the Colonial era, this wood was used to carve religious figures. In the Mayan language, cedro means "wood of the gods," and in the Quiché language "wood of the saints."

Description:

The spanish cedar tree can measure from 20 to 30 meters tall. The trunk is more than one meter in diameter, usually with thin root buttresses. The outer bark is light brown with rough fissures and the inner bark is soft pink. It is a full tree with smooth branches. Its leaves are large and drooping, made up of 10 to 30 smaller leaflets. The flowers bloom in clusters, are very small, and smell somewhat like garlic.

Its fruit is a capsule full of many winged seeds. The spanish cedar grows in the rain forests of América, from Mexico, Central América to Ecuador, Peru, Brazil and the Guyanas.

Ecological Requirements:

This tree grows best in warm, humid climates, with an annual precipitation of 1500 to 5000 mm, but it also needs a marked dry season. It grows well in altitudes from 0 to 1300 meters above sea level. Deep topsoil, preferably valley soil that is fresh and well-drained, is ideal; but this hardy tree also prospers in clay or limestone soils.

Propagation:

Two propagation methods are used: seeds and pseudo-cuttings or stumps. Seeds are harvested from December to April and may remain viable for less than a month. In a controlled cold climate, these seeds may last up to a year.

The seeds are planted in seed beds until they germinate, around 8 to 20 days; they should then be transplanted to growbags until they are planted in their final location when they are a year old. The pseudo-cuttings should be a year old before they are permanently placed. The seedlings should be placed in beds of 10 by 20 cm. These plants will reach 1.5 meters in height at 6-18 months.

Planting:

These trees should be planted 6 meters apart. In countries where *Hypsiphyla grandella* is present the seedlings should be interplanted with other trees and not more than 60 trees per hectare should be planted so as to reduce the effects of this pest.

Hypsiphyla grandella is a moth that attacks the terminal shoots of the spanish cedar, especially trees under 4 years of age. Propagation by pseudo-cutting is, therefore, recommended because growth is faster. Extensive plantations should be avoided, and intercropping is highly recommended.

Production:

As fine woods go, the cedar tree is a fast grower, up to 1.5 meters a year. From the seventh year through the tenth, the plantation should be regularly thinned and the trees may be used until they are about 40 years old. A cedar tree plantation can produce up to 13 cubic meters of wood per hectare a year, using a rotation system.

Main Uses:

Spanish cedar wood is red to light brown, fine-grained, dense, lightweight, aromatic, strong and durable; it withstands termites and is easy to work, it is used to make fine furniture, window frames, doors, walls and saunas; and it is employed for such diverse items as musical instruments, sculptures and carvings, model airplanes, handicrafts, rafts, decks, boats, parquet flooring, precision machinery, windmill parts and grandfather clocks.

A tea made from its leaves, roots and bark is a home remedy for bronchitis, dyspepsia, indigestion, fevers, diarrhea, vomiting, hemorrhages and epilepsy.

The seeds are said to be able to eliminate intestinal parasites, especially worms. And of course, it is a beautiful ornamental shade tree, whose aromatic wood contains a lightweight oil.

Cedrela odorata. Fruits.

CONACASTE
(Elephant's Ear)

The wind whipped the valleys, whilst in the
twilit forests solemn conacastes, fat and aromatic
cedars, ancient ceibas blinded by their own cotton,
capulines, ebonies,
guayacanes all came, getting ever closer and closer
to one another until they formed a thick wall of
rotting fruit and nerves, tangled roots, abandoned
nests, matted scrub, gusts of wind, and dark
indefinable stretches where the only movement was
of inert bodies, a strand of white smoke, blood, and
far beyond, what seemed the roar of an angry sea.

Hombres de Maíz
Miguel Angel Asturias

Botanical name:

Enterolobium cyclocarpum (Jacq.) Griseb.

Family:

Mimosaceae (Leguminosae)

Synonyms:

Feuilleea cyclocarpa (Jacq.) Kuntze

Inga cyclocarpa (Jacq.) Willd.

Mimosa cyclocarpa Jacq.

Mimosa parota Sessé & Moc.

Common Names:

Conacaste, Guanacaste, Pit (Huehuetenango).
Elephant's ear, Monkey ear.

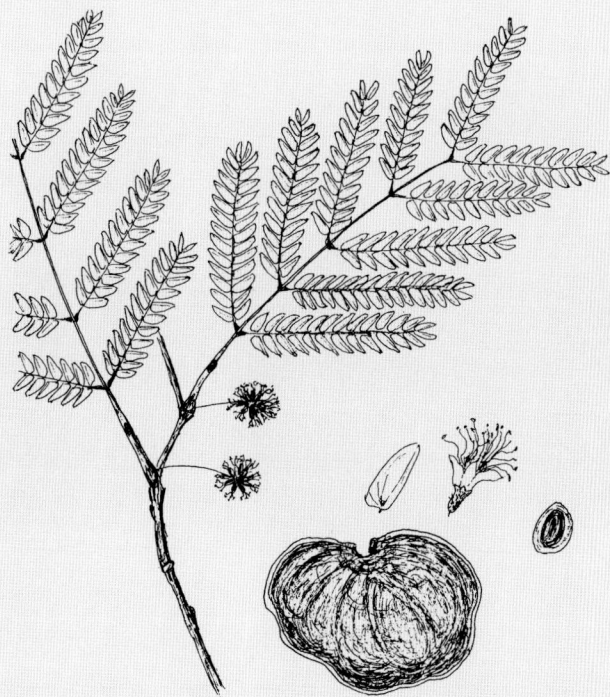

The Conacaste in Traditional Lore:

Conacaste, or elephant's ear, is one of the 4 or 5 largest trees in Central América, and also one of the best-known. It is a true giant, rivaling the ceiba (silk cotton tree) in size. The graceful, fern-like leaves of conacaste fold at night, and the foliage is very attractive, especially when the young leaves are coming out at the end of the dry season.

The word "Conacaste" is derived from Náhuatl and signifies "Trees of Ears." Two villages, in Guatemala are named after conacaste: one in El Progreso and another in Escuintla. It has also given its local name (Guanacaste) to a province of Costa Rica where it is the national tree.

Conacaste is native to Central América, from southern Mexico to Colombia. It is common in the Caribbean and has been introduced in Asia. In Guatemala, it is found on the Pacific plains, in the Motagua River valley, along small streams in Petén, Alta and Baja Verapaz, in the eastern departments, in the capital district, and in San Marcos.

Description:

Conacaste can be as tall as 30 meters and the trunk diameter can measure up to 2 meters. The crown is very broad and extensive. The greenish brown bark has many lenticels (which are spongy areas, serving as pores to permit gas exchange between the trunk and the atmosphere). The leaves are composed of numerous leaflets. The flowers are white and are grouped in small capitula (heads). The fruit, a brown, woody coiled pod, looks like a human ear and contains 10 to 15 large seeds. The wood is light brown with a fine, darker grain and, it is compact, durable, strong, and relatively light.

Ecological Requirements:

Conacaste hails from hot, semi-humid regions where the dry season is long (it survives in dry areas) and thrives in humid areas at elevations of less than 300 meters. It requires well-drained soils and prefers neutral, not acidic ones.

Propagation:

Conacaste can be easily reproduced by seed, which is gathered between February and June. A pound of seed contains anywhere from 500 to 1500 seeds. Seeds can be treated in one of 3 ways to facilitate germination: 1) Using sand paper, part of the seed coat, on the opposite side to the radicle, is worn away. Only the integument should be filed down, the seeds are then soaked in water for 24 hours. 2) Letting the seeds soak in initially boiling water for 1 or 2 days, they will germinate within 4 days. 3) Soaking the seeds for 60 minutes in 50% or 70% (by weight) sulphuric acid, which is then neutralized by adding an appropriate base, such as lime wash. The seeds are then washed and planted.

If the soil contains enough moisture, the seeds can be planted directly, otherwise they can be put in large grow bags. Conacaste can also be propagated by stem cuttings; these are cared for in a nursery for 12 to 14 weeks, and then transplanted to the field. The tree does not grow well in the shade and prefers full sunlight.

Planting:

For wood production, conacaste trees can be planted 3 or 4 meters apart. When planted this close together, the trees grow quite straight. If *E. cyclocarpum* is planted to provide shade, a distance of 20 meters or more between trees is sufficient because the crowns become very wide.

Conacaste is fast-growing and can grow 2 to 3 meters a year, and the trunk diameter can increase by 10 centimeters annually.

Main Uses:

Conacaste wood is beautiful, easy to work , and easy to finish. It dries well with the help of good ventilation. Valued as highly as cedar wood, conacaste is used for construction, cabinetwork, decorative objects, floors, boards, panels for rural buildings, veneers, plywood, carts and wheels. It is made into mortars for husking rice and coffee beans, trays,

washing boards, and, due to its water resistance, it is used to make dug-out canoes, which are usually quite large. The wood has a moderate resistance to decaying actions of bacteria and fungi and to termites. Conacaste is also used as firewood.

The seeds are edible after being shelled and toasted and with a protein content of up to 36%, they are very nutritious. The leaves and green pods with 17% protein are a useful protein source for livestock. Conacaste is an excellent shade tree for cattle ranches, but because of its large size, it is not as suitable for plantations. In Mexico, the juice of the pods is used to form charcoal dust into "cakes," which produce a lot of heat on burning. In Guatemala, the young pods are used as a soap substitute. Sap from the conacaste tree has medicinal properties (it relieves bronchitis), and tannins from the bark are used for curing hides.

Conacaste is cultivated for shade and ornamental purposes, particularly on pasture grounds and along roads. It is a melliferous tree (producing honey). The sawdust from conacaste wood causes nasal allergies and itching, and, if the sawdust is dumped into rivers, it can kill fish.

Enterolobium cyclocarpum. Flowers.

CHICOZAPOTE

(Sapodilla)

Throughout those endless days and the lugubrious nights,
Valentín and Jorge lived the sad life that the gum tappers live.
It was an extremely difficult and painful job,
beneath the torture of mosquitos
and the constant rainstorms,
because it was when it was raining
that the gum trickled down more abundantly.
They left their bags by the trunks of the trees at night...
The mosquitos followed them inseparably,
sucking the blood from their bodies
right through their sweaty clothes.
They made the trees bleed
and the mosquitos did the same to them.
This was the compensating law of the jungle.

Guayacán
Virgilio Rodríguez Macal

Botanical name:

Manilkara zapota (L.) P. Royen

Family:

Sapotaceae

Synonyms:

Achras zapota L.
Achras zapotilla (Jacq.) Nutt.
Manilkara achras (Mill.) Fosberg
Manilkara zapotilla Gilly
Sapota achras Mill.

Common names:

Chicozapote, Chico, Zapotillo, Zapote-chico ("Little Zapote") Zapote (Petén), Ya' (Maya), Mui (Q'eqchi'). Tzaput (K'iche'), White Zapote, Coloured Zapote, Sapotilla.
Sapodilla tree, Chewing gum tree, Naseberry, Dilly.

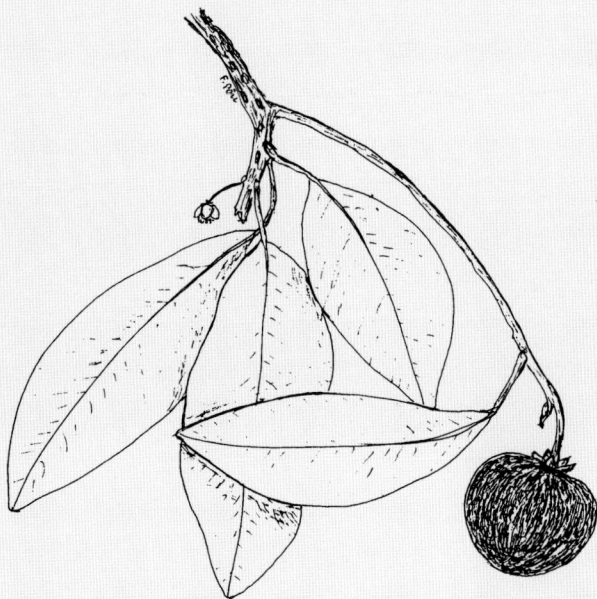

The Chicozapote in Traditional Lore:

The sapodilla tree was discovered during the first Spanish explorations, and was soon distributed around the world. Its wood, known for its strength and durability, was used extensively by the Maya in their temples and other large buildings. An example of this is a carved lintel from Temple 4 in Tikal. The original, which dates from 350 A.D., was taken to Basel, Switzerland in the 1870s. The classic Maya also chewed gum made from the milky juice of the sapodilla tree.

The sapodilla tree, from which chicle (gum) is tapped, has played an integral part in the socio-economic make-up of Petén and Guatemala, because of the previous importance of the chewing gum industry. The virtual extinction of the Lacandones ("the true people"), the most direct descendants of the Maya (in Lacandón language chicle is called "ya'"), was mainly the result of the exploitation of this tree.

All species of the Sapotaceae family produce a milky latex; however, the quantity and quality produced by the various members of this family differ.

The world's largest commercial plantations of sapodilla are probably found in Central América and Mexico. The sapodilla was one of the most important trees for the Central American economy, providing one of the principal export products, the gum from which all chewing gums are made. Most of the gum was produced in Petén, Belize, and parts of the Yucatán peninsula, where at one time there were an estimated 100 million trees of this species. During the period when chicle production was at its height, from 1927 to 1929, 12 million pounds were produced annually. The sap of other members of the Sapotaceae family was used for diluting genuine chicle, especially in Yucatán and Northern Belize where such substitute varieties were abundant.

The Spanish common name for *Manilkara zapota*, chicozapote, is derived from the tree's Náhuatl name,

"Tzicozapotl," which means gum sapote or gum sapodilla. The sapodilla tree is native to the South of Mexico, Belize, Guatemala, and Honduras. In Guatemala it is found in the mixed forests of Petén, as well as in Baja and Alta Verapaz, where it has become acclimatized near old villages and towns. *Manilkara zapota* has spread to all the tropical countries of the American continent, as well as to India, Sri Lanka, Indonesia, the Philippines and Africa, and it is commercially important in many countries.

Description:

The sapodilla tree grows up to 40 meters tall. Its straight trunk has a diameter of up to 1 meter. The wood is dark brown, with a large quantity of vessels which conduct the latex known as chicle. The crown is wide and dense, with branches extending horizontally from the trunk in all directions. The bright green leaves are elliptic and coriaceous, between 4 and 15 cm long. Small flowers grow on the leaf axils. The fruit may vary in size and shape, it can be round or egg-shaped, with a diameter of 4 to 10 cm and when ripe, the skin is reddish brown. The thin and somewhat rough peel comes off easily. The edible part of the fruit is soft and yellowish brown, rather milky, and very sweet once it has ripened. The pulp contains up to 12 hard, flat seeds, positioned in the form of a star. The branches of the Sapodilla sometimes have a tendency to bend due to the weight of ripe fruits.

The wood is cream-colored, compact, heavy, durable, very resistant to wear and tear, and can be successfully bent with steam.

Ecological Requirements:

The sapodilla tree is very adaptable in terms of climate. It prefers a hot and humid climate (in Guatemala it typically grows in humid, warm, lowland forests) from sea level to 1000 meters; however, it adapts itself very well to a dry climate if irrigation is used. Although young sapodilla trees are sensitive to low temperatures, older trees do endure light frosts.

The sapodilla requires an annual rainfall of 1200 to 2500 mm, and a temperature between 0° and 40° C.

The trees are also quite tolerant of salty breezes which occur near beaches. They are not particular with respect to soil type and grow well in limey, rocky, sandy, or clay soils. Optimum production is obtained in loose, deep, well-drained soils with a high organic content. In sandy soils, sapodilla is at risk of being uprooted by wind.

Propagation:

Sapodilla is usually seed propagated, but a large number of clones have been created by making cuttings of cultivars originating from a single plant. Seed propagation works well, although this method is slower than vegetative propagation. Six different varieties of Sapodilla have been established so far.

Grafting of *Manilkara zapota* onto stock of the same family is also possible. In Guatemala, *Calocarpum viride* (synonym: *Pouteria viridis* [Pittier] Cronquist), is used, which produces excellent fruit and grows in temperate locations such as Palín, Jacaltenango and elsewhere.

Another effective propagation method is air layering of shoots. It takes 3 to 4 months for the layer, or stem piece, to grow roots, after which it is cut from the mother plant and transplanted to grow independently.

Planting:

The low varieties of *Manilkara zapota* which spread sidewards are planted 10 to 14 meters apart, and the tall-growing varieties can be planted at a distance of 7 to 9 meters, in plantations, agroforestry systems or family orchards. A deep hole should be dug (30 cm wide and 60 to 80 cm deep) and plenty of humus added. Small plants need protection from sunlight and wind.

Sapodilla needs little trimming. The lower branches up to 60 to 90 cm from the ground, are removed after 3 to 4 years. Pruning for fructification is not carried out because the flowers grow on new shoots. Irrigation during dry periods enhances growth, although the plants will survive without it; and they can also endure strong winds.

Application of organic fertilizers is recommended, at a rate of 40 Kg/y per tree, and 2 kilograms of super phosphate for mature trees. Up to 1 kilogram of nitrogen and 0.5 kilogram of potassium are applied each year. These amounts should be divided in two portions and applied at different times of the year. The basal shoots must be removed.

Production:

Sapodilla trees take a long time to mature. Seed-grown trees become productive after six years or more. Trees which were vegetatively propagated begin to produce after 3 years. If they flower within 3 years of planting, it is best to remove the flowers before the fruit sets.

Sapodilla is not self-pollinating (it is self-sterile). This means that different cultivars of sapodilla must grow in each other's vicinity for cross-pollination to take place. In other words, different varieties of Manilkara zapota should be planted in the same plantation to ensure that fertilization can occur and that a large crop can be produced each year. The fruit is harvested from January to April. Optimum production is obtained in hot climates without a dry season.

The fruit of sapodilla trees is attacked by fruit flies (Ceratitis capitata). Cochineal insects and caterpillars damage the leaves and shoots.

Main Uses:

The fruit is usually eaten raw. The most important product of Manilkara zapota in economic terms is chicle, the basic ingredient of chewing gum. The latex from which chicle is prepared is drawn off the cortex of the tree. It is extracted by making slanting incisions in the trunk.

Tapping should be done very carefully, as it is possible to ruin a tree by cutting too deeply.

The wood is of high quality and quite hard, which is why it is able to withstand very strong winds. It is easy to saw, and planing the wood results in a nice finish. Sapodilla wood is suitable for heavy construction and for building parts of boats that are not submerged in water. It is used for manufacturing tool handles, sports articles, musical instruments, etc. It is moderately resistant to the decaying actions of bacteria and fungi and to destructive insects. Sapodilla wood dries slowly, and its preservation requires effort and care. The bark and seeds have medicinal properties.

Manilkara zapota. Fruits.

"Chiclero" cutting the cortex to extract the gum.

Milky latex of sapodilla tree.

Sapodilla wood used in temple in Tikal.

GUANO
(Palm Tree)

...Then he saw that he was under a roof of palm,
of well plaited guano leaves. The roof was high, blackened
by smoke in the center, which pointed upwards and
outwards. Valentin's eyes looked around. It was a
spacious thatched hut, with solid columns made of irayol
wood. In fact, every single component of the construction
was made of the vegetable kingdom. The palm thatch
was tied to the roof frame with reeds, and reeds too were
used as joints and as fastenings for the columns.

Guayacán
Virgilio Rodríguez Macal

Botanical name:

Sabal mexicana Mart.

Family:

Arecaeae (Palmae)

Synonym:

Sabal guatemalensis Becc.

Common names:

Guano, Huano de Sombrero, Botán.
Palm tree, broom palm, hat palm, Palmetto,
"Big Thatch," Sabal palm.

The Guano in Traditional Lore:

This palm tree is closely linked to the Mayas due to its use in thatching roofs since pre-colonial days.

The edible hearts of *Sabal mexicana* are an important survival food in the jungle. In several regions of Petén, the palm tree was used by the Lacandones for ceremonial purposes, especially to commemorate the dead.

The most common species in this part of Central América is *Sabal mayarum*; however, it is not as prevalent as previously. *Sabal mexicana* is found throughout the Motagua Valley in El Progreso, Zacapa and Chiquimula. It usually grows in large groves near river banks and on slopes. *Sabal mexicana* also thrives in cattle pastures and in places where lumber has been harvested.

Description:

Young plants can be quite large, but with no visible stem. Older plants have a trunk 10 to 12 meters high, culminating in a crest of large, beautiful leaves. The trunk is marked with protruding rings; previous leafstalks can usually be detected below the leaves. The leaves measure approximately 1 meter by 1 meter and are divided into segments, the largest of which are 4 to 6 centimeters wide. The slender petioles are about as long as the leaves. The inflorescences are the same size, or slightly bigger than the leaves. They are compact, with smooth, thin stalks, up to 12 cm long. The off-white, fragrant flowers are 3 to 4 centimeters in diameter and have unfurled petals and cup-shaped calyxes. The petals, which are bigger than the calyxes and equal in size to the anthers, are slender, sharp-pointed and veined. The numerous fruits, which grow in clusters, measure 13 to 20 by 15 mm, and although they appear globular, they are flattened at the base. The chocolate colored seeds have a diameter of 9 mm and are flat on one side and convex on the other.

Ecological Requirements:

Sabal mexicana grows on open, dry hillsides, on coastal plains or in river valleys; sometimes it appears along the edges of mangrove or bamboo swamps. It is found from sea level to 1400 meters and flourishes in a warm climate with a precipitation from 1000 to 2000 mm per year.

Propagation:

Sabal mexicana is seed propagated. The seeds, which do not stay viable for very long, can be planted directly in the field or they can be started in a container in the nursery. Germination occurs after 60 days. Seedlings in the nursery can be transplanted after several months.

Planting:

The spacing between trees in a plantation or garden plot is about 3 meters by 8 meters.

Production:

The first crop of palm hearts can be harvested after approximately three and a half years. The hearts must be cut away very carefully, so that maximum yield is obtained without damaging the plants.

Principal Uses:

Sabal palm is usually planted as an ornamental. Its leaves are used for thatching cottage roofs and sheds in which tobacco is dried. They are also suitable for making hats and, when dry, can be made into brooms, mats, baskets, fans and other handmade objects.

The Sabal palm produces berries which ripen at the end of the rainy season, in November. Palm hearts are consumed throughout the year, but more frequently when the leaves are cut for thatching. The older the heart, the more bitter it tastes, but this bitterness disappears when the heart is roasted.

Other edible parts are the inflorescence, before it matures and while still enclosed in the spathe. Called "pacayas" in Spanish, these can be either boiled or fried and are often sprinkled with lemon juice. One frequently sees pacayas for sale in regional markets, principally in Jocotán, Chiquimula. The core of the stem of *Sabal chamaedorea* is sometimes chopped and put in a bag to ferment. Later, the resulting liquid is mixed with ginger and a drink similar to wine is prepared. Sabal palm seeds are rich in oil which is used for making soap.

Other Species:

Another species of sabal palm growing in Petén, Guatemala and Belize is *Sabal mayarum* Bartlett, which occurs at very low altitudes. *Sabal mayarum* is rather small, reaching only 4 meters in height. Its leaves can be 2 meters wide and bright green; and the incisions, which almost reach the base leaf, divide each one into many segments. The undivided part of the leaf is between 15 and 20 centimeters long. The flowers are 3 to 4 mm long.

Lacandon indians thatching a cottage roof with Sabal leaves.

101

COROZO
(Cohune)

It is marvelous to see so many different kinds of
palm trees that God has placed in this América
to enhance and widen his infinite power.

One of these palms, corozo, abounds in areas of
grassy pastures and the gulf. Its heart is easily
acquired and it produces bunches of small
"coconuts," which are called cachimbos in Brazil.

Its center seems to be an almond, and it produces
great amounts of oil that can be used as fuel for
lamps or as food.

The Natural History of the Kingdom of Guatemala
Fray Francisco Jiménez

Botanical name:

Attalea cohune Mart.

Family:

Arecaceae (Palmae)

Synonyms:

Orbignya cohune (Mart.) Dahlgren ex Standl.

Common names:

Corozo, Manaca, Tutz (Maya), Corós (Q'eqchí).
Cohune.

The Corozo in Traditional Lore:

This palm, native to the tropical rain forest, is very important because of its wide use in rural construction. The leaves provide shade and protection for local inhabitants, and the abundant fruits provide an oil that at one time was valued for industrial use, as witnessed by several processing plants that existed in the Izabal area of Guatemala. The heart of this palm is also processed and sold as an appetizer; while the shell and pit of the fruit provide excellent fuel. The moisture guarded by the trunk and branches allows many lichens and ferns to prosper, which in turn provide homes for insects, birds and small mammals such as opossums.

The corozo is the largest and most majestic palm of Central América. Its groves form a dense under-forest but can also develop well without shade, and can be observed in open spaces in any of its native areas. Leaves 10 to 12 meters in length are quite common, and they are probably the longest leaves of any American plant. Brigham, who studied this and other Guatemalan plants for many years, estimated that from the inflorescence of this palm more than 30,000 staminate flowers could appear, thus attracting large numbers of bees and wasps. In the northern coastal region of Guatemala, the lumber is used to build homes and huts; the majority of these are built almost exclusively from different parts of this plant: the frame of the structure is formed from the 'ribs' of the leaves and the roof from thatched leaves that give a dense protection. New leaves are made into hats; and in Alta Verapaz the longest folioles are sometimes plaited into suyacales, rainsheets to protect vendors and their loads from the rain, although nowadays plastic sheets are mostly used. Suyates, a kind of thin mattress, are made from the brownish leaf petioles and, then are used as bedding and as mats under donkey and horse saddles.

Description:

The corozo is a large palm, frequently trunkless or with a very short one. Adult trees are from 9 to 15 meters in height and often persistent leaf bases may be found in the higher sections. The leaves are shaped like very graceful, curved feathers with many elongated segments, and are often quite large, 10 meters long and 2 meters wide. The male staminate inflorescence usually measures 1 to 1.5 meters long, covered by many tiny male flowers. The female flowers are large, almost balloonish. The fruit clusters hang large and heavy; they usually carry from 800 to 1000 fruits, which can each measure up to 6 cm long and look like small coconuts. Each palm tree produces large quantities of nuts, and a fruit cluster can weigh more than 100 pounds.

Ecological Needs:

The corozo is common along the Atlantic coast, and can be found in the departments of Petén, Alta Verapaz and Izabal. It is also found in Belize, and from southeaster Mexico to Honduras and south to Costa Rica.

The corozo usually prospers in well-drained soils, be they flat or sloping, at 300 meters above sea level or less. The corozo needs a warm and humid climate, fresh soils rich in organic material and full sunlight. It is very resistant to fire and drought (withstands up to 4 to 6 months), and can prosper in the poor soils of the savannas, with a rainfall of 1000 to 2000 mm per year.

Propagation:

The shell of the seed is very thick and hard, and if not attacked by beetle larvae, the seed can remain latent for years. Sometimes heat or fire is needed to interrupt this lethargy; but the seeds, once separated, sprout after several months. Their growth is slow; a strong and penetrating main root sprouts first, followed by other smaller roots and a stem. Growth in nurseries is troublesome because large bags are needed from the very beginning. The plants bear fruit from their eighth to twelfth year when they reach a height of 8 meters; and they can produce up to 1500 kilos of nuts a year per hectare. This is a palm tree that grows very slowly; its seeds take from 8 to 18 months to sprout when they are in favorable conditions, which include a humid climate and organically enriched soil. The flowers are protected by a thick-skinned giant, maroon spathe, 5 to 7 feet long. Root transplants have been effected: it is very important to protect these from direct sunlight for a certain amount of time; the leaves may droop, but at four months the sprouts will revive. The fruits, abundant year round, take 6 months to ripen, when they fall from the cluster.

Main Uses:

Corozo seed is very important and has a flavor similar to coconut. The seed is 65% oil, which is used for cooking and soap making. The fruit is eaten raw. The only obstacle to the growth of the corozo industry is the hardness of the nuts making them difficult to process.

Indigenous workers thatching a cottage roof with *Attalea* leaves.

MANGLE
(Mangrove)

Take me,
warm current,
wrap me in your seductive mantle,
drag me to your magnificent domains
where the sky touches the sea
and where the sea is formed of a river
of sensual sensations
left in oblivion.

Warm Feelings
Enrique Carredano

Botanical name:

Rhizophora mangle L.

Family:

Rhizophoraceae

Synonym:

Rhizophora samoensis (Hochr.) Salvoza

Common names:

Mangle, Mangle Rojo, Mangle Colorado, Tapche, Tabche.

Mangrove.

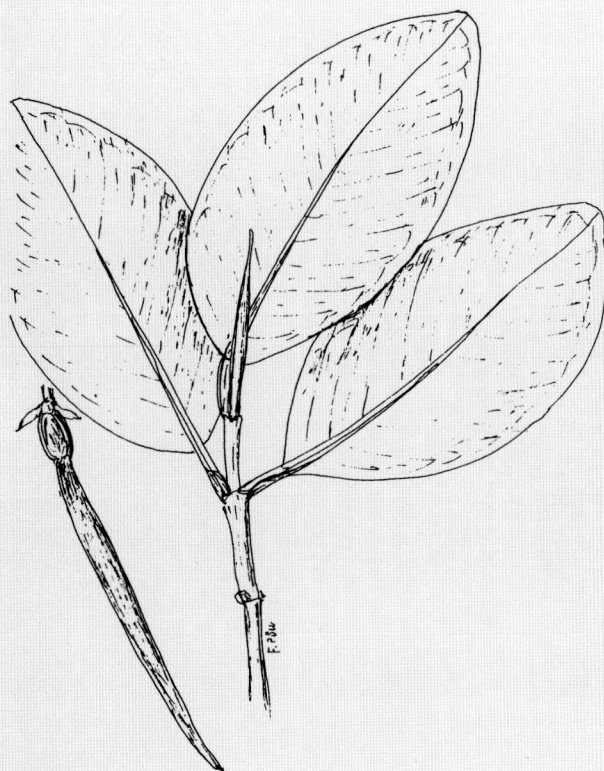

The Mangle in Traditional Lore:

Mangrove are very important for the life cycles of many crustaceans, mussels and small fish, and is basic to the development of aquaculture industries. By eating its leaves, small microorganisms initiate the food chain in the estuary ecosystem.

Description:

Trees can be from 10 to 25 meters high, and at least 60 cm in diameter. The tree shaft does not touch the soil; is cylindrical in shape and very straight. The roots are aerial, visible and help support the tree. Its bark can be gray or grayish brown and is smooth to the touch. The crown is irregular and sparse, made up of simple, opposite, elliptical, shiny green leaves. Its flowers are small and yellowish-green. The brown or green fruit is cone-shaped long and leathery. The seed is large, germinates on the tree and is dispersed by water currents.

Ecological Requirements:

The mangrove is semi-aquatic; it adapts naturally to tidal flooding and the overflowing of rivers. Its ideal habitat is in bay areas, where rivers run smoothly into the sea. The mangrove tree grows only in semi-tropical and tropical regions because it requires high temperatures. The minimum annual rainfall required by the mangrove is 1000 mm; and it reproduces better in very moist soil as found in swamps or channels. The red mangrove lives in brackish water, in waters that are regularly flooded by ocean tides, and also in fresh water. High salt concentrations curb its growth. However, at least some salinity is necessary for part of the year.

Propagation:

The mangrove seed is called candelilla. This seed sprouts on the tree, but must ripen; if harvested before time, it is useless. Seeds should be collected from the beaches or swamps.

Planting:

The seed should be planted directly in soil free from refuse and the roots of any other species. They should be planted 40 cm apart, 80 cm between each row. After 12 years, the young mangrove should be redistributed. Dams and dikes can reduce the forest's productivity and may even destroy it.

Production:

The density of a mangrove forest varies but is usually between 600 to 800 plants per hectare. Commercial plantations usually produce around 400 cubic meters per hectare after 25 years. The mangrove sprouts from the end of each branch and excessive pruning may annihilate the tree. It is very resistant to pests and disease.

Main Uses:

The wood of the mangrove tree is red or reddish-brown with gray or pink yellow rays streaming from the center. It has an irregular grain and is very resistant to the wear and tear of nature and pests. It is highly esteemed in agro industries and widely used in rural housing. In heavy construction this wood is used for rafters, supporting pillars, posts and docks, tool handles, furniture and firewood. The bark is used as a dye for cloth and also for tanning leather. Upon boiling, the bark produces a healing tea that can lower fevers, and check hemorrhage and diarrhea.

The mangrove provides natural protection against tidal waves, typhoons and tropical storms, and stabilizes coastal sands and soil formations.

Rhizophora mangle.

Wood continues to be an essential component of the constructions and furnishings used by the inhabitants of the area. It is also commonly used to manufacture tools, handicrafts and utensils, in a fashion very similar to that used in ancient Maya urban centers.

Trees as Firewood

Wood as a source of energy has been very important in the Maya World. Many questions have not been answered concerning the collapse of such a great civilization. Could over explotation of the natural resources have caused it?

Trees as Firewood

The Maya people of Guatemala depend largely on firewood to prepare meals and as a heat source. Cooking the "tortillas" and black beans with fire is an ancestral tradition. This has caused a lot of deforestation.

While on a small scale, firewood is a renewable resource, large scale use of wood for fuel can lead to deforestation. Alternatives such as solar and geothermal energy need to be employed to arrest deforestation. Trees used as a source of energy include pine, leucaena, and oak.

The fast growing leucaena was well known by the pre-Colombian people of Mexico and Central América. It is also used as a "living tutor" of different crops, providing shade, protection against the wind, and improving the soil due to its ability to fix nitrogen.

Pine and oak are possibly the most characteristic Guatemalan trees and for this reason, the most frequently used. They grow in the entire mountain chain that traverses the country and at various altitudes, usually in mixed forests. Pine is extensively used in rural construction and carpentry.

Oaks also provide a rich compost and the tiny acorns are an important food source for wildlife, mammals and many colorful birds that inhabit the forests. They also support hundred of epiphytes, such as orchids, bromeliads and ferns.

ENCINO
(Oak)

There are many oaks in the high areas, but not as those
found in Spain, but rather holly oaks; and their fruits
are small bitter acorns something like holly berries.
The wood is good only for burning,
and because of the hollow spaces, many bees live in
these trees and build their hives in the trunks.

The Natural History of the Kingdom of Guatemala
Fray Francisco Ximénez

Botanical name:

Quercus spp.

Family:

Fagaceae

Common names:

Encino, Roble.

Oak.

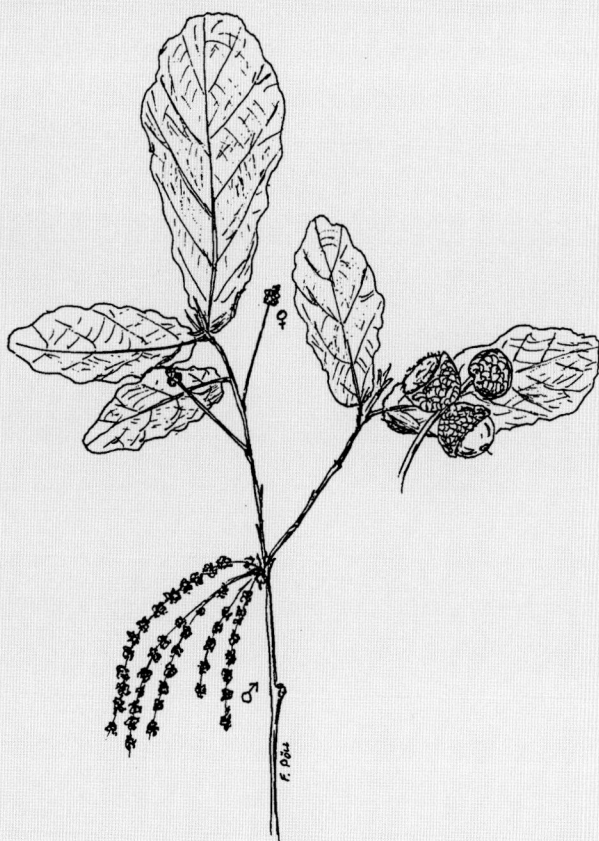

The Encino in Traditional Lore:

The oak tree is the main source of organic energy for the Guatemalan population. This timber is preferred for firewood because of its long duration and high heat, and due to this the oak forests are constantly plundered. The oak genus, *Quercus* is very extensive and although the exact number of species is not known, it is thought to be between 200 and 370 in the American continent. Muller asserted that 46 of these are native to Central América, and within these the majority are from Guatemala, even though several species prosper in Costa Rica and Panama.

Guatemalan oaks originally covered large portions of the highlands and eastern regions. Oaks and pine trees are native and important to the country, and almost all the forests are a combination of these species. Nevertheless, pure oak forests can be found, and it is thought that oak trees once completely covered the moderate elevations of the arid mountains.

The most extensive tracts of oak trees in the country can be found on the almost barren mountains of Baja Verapaz. There are also large numbers in the dense, mixed forests of the Pacific plains and on the steep volcanic slopes. Oaks also grow at moderate and even high altitudes in Quetzaltenango and San Marcos regions. Unfortunately, these forests have been greatly reduced in size due to an increasing demand for firewood and timber, and advancing agriculture.

Around Quetzaltenango and Cerro Quemado, the oak leaf is used as a natural fertilizer for the barren lands of the mountain slopes.

All oak seeds, or acorns, can be eaten, but some species are very bitter. The seeds of some white oaks are somewhat sweet and have a pleasant flavor. These nuts were an important food source for some North American native tribes, but not for the Central American tribes, although it is thought that in times of starvation acorns may have been eaten in Guatemala.

Description:

The oak can be a medium to large sized tree, from 6 to 30 m tall or occasionally a shrub. The alternate leaves are wide, almost always petiolate, serrated, persistent or deciduous, with male staminate blooms as hanging catkins. There are few female blooms, and these are arranged in short catkins.

The fruit is an acorn, which sits in a cup formed by female bloom branches. This cup can cover the acorn, completely or partially.

Ecological Needs:

The majority of these subtropical species are originally from mountain areas; but different species can be found at altitudes from 300 meters (*Q. oleifolia*) to 3000 meters (*Q. acatenangensis*).

It would be interesting to include these trees in more trial plantings.

Propagation:

There are between 100 to 1500 acorns per kilo of seeds; this amount varies according to species. Seeds can germinate up to three months after collecting and can be conserved in the refrigerator at one to four degrees Centigrade. They should be planted immediately. They can be planted in growbags, or in nurseries, and will sprout at four to eight weeks. They also can sprout in water and then be planted in the ground or a growbag. Seeds that float on the surface should be rejected.

The harvest of the oak tree for firewood and fodder purposes is rotated in short time spans, and trees will resprout well. Each tree can produce from 30 to 40 kilos of fodder a year (Nepal). The date of harvest changes according to the species. There are ripe acorns from April to January; because

of this, it is very important to record the date of harvest of each specific area. The acorns are ready when they begin to fall off the trees, and many are lost because they are eaten by the local wildlife.

Main Uses:

The genus *Quercus* is most important for firewood and lumber production. The wood is well-known for its strength, lasting durability and beauty. Its use is widespread:

Railroad and ship supports, flooring, decorations and furniture. The wood of each species is different and varies in physical qualities; some are hard and resistant, others are very light, soft and less resistant. The fruit is usually an excellent food source for hogs. The acorns of some species are roasted for human consumption. All produce pollen for honey and by providing support for hundreds of epiphyts species, they are important in maintaining diversity.

The bark is rich in tannic acid which is used to treat the thickest and most durable leathers. In Guatemala, the bark is used to tan leathers, and also produces a brown dye used in textiles. These trees may have small tumor shaped lesions (galls) that are caused by insects. An infusion of oak leaves and/or bark is used as a home remedy and as an astringent. It is also used as a mouth wash when a person is suffering from toothache. The ashes produced by burning the wood are used as lye in soapmaking.

Species:

Twenty-six species and two varieties of *Quercus* have been reported in Guatemala.

Some species found in Guatemala:
Quercus acatenangensis Trel.
 Quercus peduncularis Née
Quercus pilicaulis Trel.
Quercus purulhana Trel.
Quercus skinneri Benth.

LEUCAENA
(Wild Tamarind)

You were a seed
and the restless breeze of the immense valley took you
and there the transparent rainwater baptized you.
You were born there without troubles or fears
searching for God in your blooming ascent
and there you drank of the air of life
with the green lungs of your leaves.

To A Tree
Emiro Funsanta

Botanical name:

Leucaena leucocephala (Lam.) de Wit

Family:

Mimosaceae (Leguminosae)

Synonyms:

Acacia glauca Willd.

Leucaena glauca Benth.

Mimosa glauca L.

Mimosa leucocephala Lam.

Common names:

Leucaena, Guaje, Sipia, Yaje, Huaje, Vaxi, Yage, Huaxin, Barba de León, Tamarindillo, Barcillo Hediondilla, Lino, Aroma blanca, Aroma boba, Panelo. Wild Tamarind.

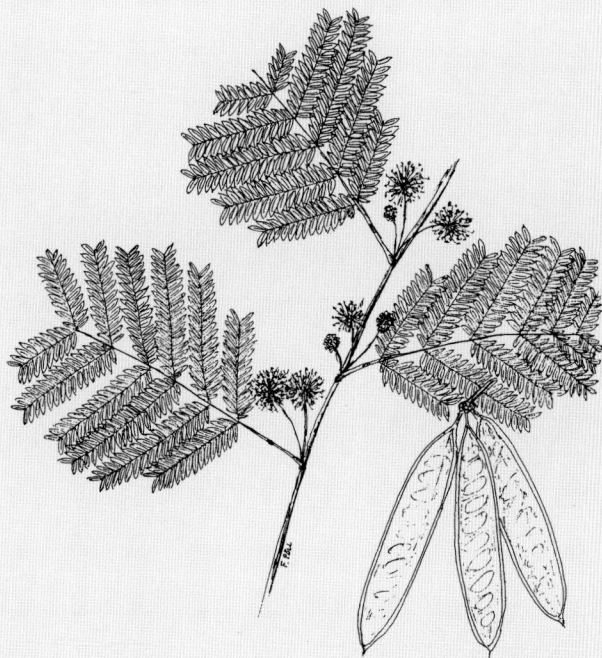

The Leucaena in Traditional Lore:

This species has been known since Pre Colombian times. Its name comes from the Mexican city of Oaxaca. After the conquest of Mexico, the Spanish took the tree to the Philippines and then to Indonesia, Malaysia, New Guinea and southeast Asia.

Due to its rapid growth and nitrogen fixation, this species has been used successfully in reforestation because it enriches the soil, especially in eroded areas. Its ripe seeds are used in local handicrafts to produce necklaces and bracelets. In the northern Huehuetenango regions of Chicáj and Nentón, the green seeds are eaten and can be used as a delousing remedy for children.

Description:

Leucaena, or wild tamarind, is a shrub or small tree from 5 to 20 meters high (usually between 6 and 12 meters). Its trunk is cylindrical, twisted and full of branches; it measures around 25 cm in diameter and branches out at several levels. The bark is smooth, spotted and gray to gray-brown.

The leaves are alternate, bipinnate, from 10 to 20 cm long with 3 to 10 pairs of leaflets, and at the last pair they may have a gland. The leaflets are made up of 10 to 20 pairs of smaller leaflets. The inflorescence are heads, 1.5 to 3 cm in diameter, with axilary and terminal peduncles.

The fruits are flat linear pods that measure about 20 cm long and 2 cm wide containing around 15 to 20 seeds. Bunches of 15 to 60 green pods will turn brown as they ripen. The seeds are shiny brown and slightly elliptical in shape measuring 3 to 4 mm wide and 1 cm long.

The wood is light yellow; the heartwood gradually changes color from yellow brown to dark brown, and is odorless and tasteless. The grain is fine, easy to finish and polish.

The roots can extend 2 meters down in one year, and up to 5 meters in 5 years. It also has the special capacity of fixing nitrogen.

The species, *L. leucocephala,* has several variants in its growth habits and these have been classified in three groups:

Hawaiian type: This 5 meter high shrub originally comes from the Yucatán peninsula. It blooms early in its lifetime, and its production of lumber and leaves is slight.

Salvadorean type: This taller and very productive tree originated in Central América. It can grow up to 20 m tall. Its leaves are long, with thick branches. It is used for timber, lumber and pulp.

Peruvian type: The origin of this type is not clear. It can grow up to 15 meters tall with a short trunk and many branches. In Guatemala, it grows well in Izabal, Zacapa, Escuintla, Santa Rosa, Retalhuleu and Suchitepéquez.

Ecological Requirements:

The limiting factors in the spread of this tree are rainfall and altitude. It grows well at low elevations, from sea level to 1000 meters; in both dry and humid areas with up to 2300 mm of annual rainfall. It can survive droughts of 3 to 6 months, but frost kills it. It adapts well to areas that maintain an average temperature of 16 to 32 degrees Centigrade (coastal zones and lower altitude regions). The soil should be well-drained and compact; it grows well in moderately acid soils and alkaline soils. To grow well the tree needs the elements calcium, phosphorus and sulfur.

Propagation:

The tree can reproduce by seed or pseudo-cuttings. If done by seed, these are harvested by hand from April to May. A kilogram of seeds has around 18,000 units, which can be saved for several years. The tree produces an abundant amount of fruit and is easily harvested.

The pods should be collected when they have turned brown. New seeds sprout naturally; if they have been saved for a year or more, they should be treated with 80° C hot water for two to three minutes, or boiling water for 30 seconds and then placed in cold water for a day. They can be planted in their final site in growbags or in nursery beds at a depth of one cm. They will sprout in 4 to 10 days. The seedlings planted in growbags will reach 30 to 50 cm in three or four months. Then they can be transplanted. To repopulate a difficult forest area, pseudo-cuttings are recommended. These are planted in rows 20 to 30 cm apart in beds. They should reach from 50 to 80 cm in height and 1 to 1.5 cm in diameter. These cuttings should have a root of 20 to 30 cm long and an average height of 15 cm. This can be attained by trimming the cutting. The roots can also be planted directly in the definitive site.

Main Uses:

The lumber of this tree is mainly used for flooring, parquet, tabletops, carpentry, small wooden articles, boxes and crates, electricity and telephone posts, beams and supports for mine excavations, framework for plant support such as bananas, pulp and paper, firewood and charcoal and the preparation of alcohol fuel.

Because the leaves contain from 20 to 30% raw protein and are rich in amino acids, calcium and phosphorus, they are widely used as fodder. Unfortunately, they also produce a toxic alkaloid called mimosina that affects non-ruminant mammals (horses, hogs and rabbits) and may even affect ruminant mammals if excessive amounts are consumed.

Trees as Medicine

The answers to the horrible plagues of our times might be hidden in the forest. There is still much to be revealed. Fortunately, as a new century begins, a conscious part of humankind is searching in ancient wisdom for clues to a sound relationship with the planet and all its treasures. The medicinal virtues of plants are Earth's biggest gift: health is the soul of life.

Trees as Medicine

The healing virtues of trees as well as of many other plants were well known to the ancient Maya and they continue to be utilized by their descendants, although the influence of western medicine has led to a decline in the use of these valuable traditional remedies. Hopefully, a growing interest in alternative and traditional medicine, both locally and world-wide, can demonstrate the importance of this field before both forests and knowledge are lost. Forests hold an infinity of cures. Many have been applied for centuries by the indigenous people, many have yet to be discovered.

Many trees of the Maya World are known for their medicinal applications. The esquisúchil has been considered sacred since pre-Colombian times. The Aztec emperor Moctezuma won a war against the Pipil nation to obtain esquisúchiles to plant in his botanical garden. The tree was so precious to the indigenous peoples of Mesoamérica that the Spaniards used it as a means to lure them to specific areas. The city of Esquipulas, Guatemala, site of a famous basílica and home of the Central American Parliament, received its name from this tree. Two esquisúchiles stand peacefully in the gardens of the impressive church. The leaves and the aromatic white flowers are used against heart disease, nervous disorders, and menstrual pains. It is believed to have anti-cancerous properties and serves as a pain relief and sudorific. The sap is applied against toothache; the bark provides a cure against stomachache and rheumatism.

The properties of the guayacán were well known by the Maya. Francisco Ximénez, a Spanish friar who wrote the Natural History of Guatemala during the 1700s, describes this tree as "very recognized for its medicinal uses."

Three other trees known world wide for their healing properties are elder, logwood and liquidambar. Elderberries are extremely rich in vitamin C; they are frequently used to make jam, wine and vinegar. Both the berries and the flowers are boiled into a syrup against cough and colds; they also serve to stimulate the appetite. Logwood has traditionally been used in Mesoamérica to treat diarrhea; at present it is an official drug in the United States, where it is prescribed for the same purpose. The graceful liquidambar, or sweet gum, of the eastern cloud forests provides a balsam used in Europe to treat muscular and articular pain. Besides applying its amber sap as a balsam, the Maya mixed it with tobacco to improve effectiveness and obtained incense by letting it dry. Today, the indigenous people of the region chew on the hardened sap to polish their teeth. They also apply the balsam to heal wounds of both people and animals.

ESQUISÚCHIL

Esquisúchil tree
tired and ill,
whose leaves, lashes of your eyes,
slowly fall through time,
whose tiny blossoms, miraculous and white,
are scarce, scarcer every day.

Miraculous Esquisúchil tree
you are infested, full of stains and fungus,
gray moss on your hair,
and on your arm's clothing.
Who is your mainstay, who holds you up,
Esquisúchil tree?

The tree that was planted...
Brother Pedro José de Betancur
in his youth, straight and slim,
lived in your majestic temple.

The Esquisúchil Tree
María de la Luz Samayoa Morales

Botanical name:

Bourreria huanita (Lex.) Hemsl.

Family:

Boraginaceae

Synonyms:

Bourreria formosa (DC.) Hemsl.

Bourreria grandiflora Bertol.

Ehretia formosa DC.

Morelosia huanita Lex.

Common names:

Esquisúchil, Esquisuncha, Esquisunchil, Pepenance, Oreja de León, Árbol del Hermano Pedro.

Brother Peter's Tree.

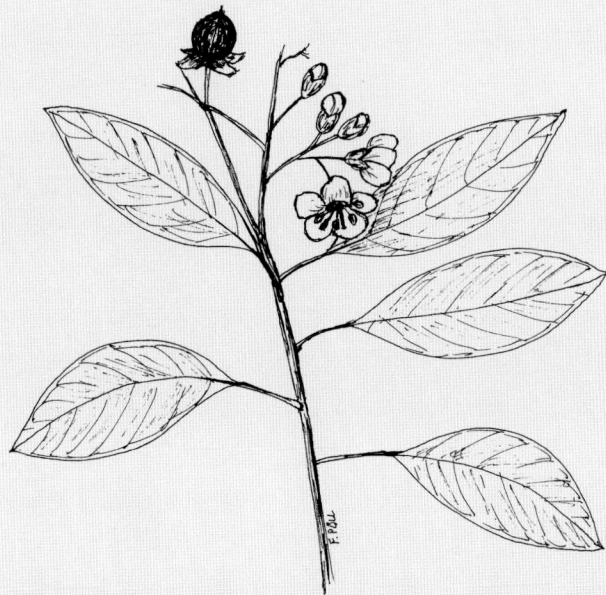

The Esquisúchil in Traditional Lore:

This tree is completely Mesoamerican. In the Natural History of New Spain, the native Mesoamerican flora is described in great detail, including the esquisúchil tree. Depending upon the country, this tree plays a different ethnic and botanical role. In Mexico, the Pipil and Aztec nations fought a war over these trees. The Aztec Emperor Moctezuma wanted to possess esquisúchil trees, sacred to the Pipil nation, and had them transplanted to his private botanical garden, but they did not survive. It is believed that the Spanish used these trees to lure the indigenous peoples to specific areas.

In El Salvador, this tree is known as Listón; a very aromatic beverage is made from mixture of its flowers and sugar.

In Guatemala, the esquisúchil tree has a very special significance as it is intimately tied to religious history. In 1657, Brother Pedro de San José Betancur is thought to have planted a cutting of an esquisúchil tree in the patio of El Calvario, a church in Antigua Guatemala. This small cutting grew into a tree that is still alive today; the flowers of this tree, according to believers, are said to have medicinal properties. In the Antigua area, esquisúchiles are cultivated in San Juan del Obispo, San Pedro Las Huertas, and San Cristóbal el Alto.

At Esquipulas, a shrine widely visited by Central American tourists, there are two flowering esquisúchil trees in the basilica garden. It is said that the name Esquipulas comes from the Náhuatl word Izquixchitl; it was here that the first steps for the Peace Treaty of Guatemala were made.

Description:

There are 3 varieties of esquisúchil trees in Guatemala. Each one may be distinguished by flower size and shape, a simple or double corolla, wide or narrow; and the form of the large fruits, which can be round or oval. There is no information regarding morphological variants of this plant in other countries. These medium-sized trees have a smooth trunk. The leaves are also smooth or with scarce short hairs. The trees are definitely elliptical or round at their top, and may be slim or oblique at their trunk. The tree blooms profusely, producing small white flowers.

Ecological Requirements:

The esquisúchil tree grows in rain forests, from sea level to 2000 meters, although its most favorable altitude is above 1000 meters.

Propagation:

A distinct characteristic of the esquisúchil tree is its difficult propagation. The seeds are generally sterile. The surest way to reproduce the tree is through radicle shoots; these appear at a certain time, and are very scarce. If the soil surrounding the tree is undisturbed, the shoots will easily sprout. The species is considered to be in danger of extinction due to the eradication of its natural habitat and the difficulty in its propagation.

Main Uses:

In Guatemala, a tea brewed from leaves or dried flowers is used to cure heart ailments and nervous disorders, and may be used as an eye wash. It may also be used as an analgesic for menstrual pains, and as an anti-abortive. It is said to have cancer fighting properties. Its flowers are very sweetly perfumed, even if dry. Its wood is used as firewood.

Bourreria huanita. Flowers.

PALO DE JIOTE

The name given to this tree, which in other tongues is called Muliche and in yet others, Caliche, is the palo de xiote because its bark peels and pustules appear, as if the tree were suffering from pox. It is a very refreshing tree. And the infusion of its bark is admirable to bathe open sores that result from heat. Its trunk is very flexible, and its only practical use is for hedges as it takes very easily. Also its sap is similar to incense.

The Natural History of the Kingdom of Guatemala
Fray Francisco Ximénez

Botanical name:

Bursera simaruba (L.) Sarg.

Family:

Burseraceae

Synonyms:

Bursera gummifera L.

B. ovalifolia (Schltdl.) Engl.

Elaphrium ovalifolium Schltdl.

E. simaruba (L.) Rose

Pistacia simaruba L.

Common names:

Jiote, Chinacauite, Palo Jiote, Solpieem, Cajha, Xacago-que (Huehuetenango), Palo Chicho Chacah, Chacah Colorado (Petén, Maya), Chaca (Huehuetenango), Palo Mulato (Petén), Indio Desnudo (costa norte), Chino (Zacapa y Chiquimula), Chic-Chica, Chicah (Petén), Cacah (Q'eqchí), Palo Santo, Palo Chino, Palo Mulato, Palo de Incienso (Central América).

Pox tree, Incense tree, Gum Elemi, Gumbo limbo, West indian birch, Birch (Belize).

The Palo de Jiote in Traditional Lore:

In Guatemala, the usual name for this tree is "palo de jiote," a word that comes from the Náhuatl dialect, because the bark gradually blisters and peels off, similar to the skin afflictions impetigo and ringworm, both of which are commonly known as "jiote." A small village in the department of Jutiapa is also called El Jiote.

The resinous sap that seeps from any cut on the tree has many applications: it was formerly used as gum arabic to repair ceramics, porcelain and glass; as protective coating for lumber used in shipbuilding; as incense and, after being boiled and left to harden, as a lacquer.

To separate the resin from the sap, the latter is collected drop by drop into gourds, then boiled in water so that the resin floats and can be easily skimmed off and dropped into cold water to harden. Later, this resin is shaped into hard but brittle blocks, wrapped in corn husks sealed with "shilote" and taken to market to be sold as incense (copal).

The people of the Caribbean coast use this same resin to paint their canoes and protect them from rot. It is thought that the word "gumbolimbo," the Belize term for the tree, may derive from the name "gomi elemi," a Spanish word for resin. In the Chortí' area the resin also has ceremonial use, as it is shaped into small coin-shaped disks, or "pesos," offered as ritual payment to their gods and also offered to the saints in Catholic churches.

The Palo de Jiote has several medicinal uses - as a laxative, a diuretic, and a sudorific, and as an antidote for snakebite. Prepared as poultices, the leaves may help reduce the spread of gangrene.

Description:

The Palo de Jiote is a straight tree that can measure up to 20 or 30 m high and has a very large crown. It has a sturdy, shiny red trunk and the bark peels off in sections.

The leaves are small, close together, and deciduous during the dry season. Its fruits are reddish-brown slightly triangular capsules about 1 cm long. The seeds are dispersed by birds.

The Palo de Jiote is native to the American tropics and can be found from southern Mexico to northern South América, as well as in the Caribbean islands and southern Florida. It grows in almost all departments of Guatemala, but especially in the Atitlán area close to Cerro de Oro and the San Lucas Tolimán Bay.

Ecological Requirements:

The tree grows well in tropical climates in primary forests, but its preferred environment is secondary forests, dry, humid or with scrub. It is more frequently found at altitudes below 1000 meters, although it can range up to 1800 meters above sea level. It needs an annual rainfall between 500 and 1400 mm and can withstand long dry spells. It tolerates salty terrain and can adapt to any variety of soils, including alkaline.

Propagation:

This tree spreads mainly by seeds but also can be planted by large cuttings (1.50 to 2.50 meters). These cuttings sprout rapidly. The trees are usually planted at low elevations, but can prosper at intermediate ones. Because the branches grow quickly as if they were on an adult tree, they are frequently used as fence posts or even as hedges. If planted close together they form a barrier and can also provide shade and charm.

Main Uses:

Besides the resin, the lumber of the Palo de Jiote is very important because it is easy to work. The wood is yellowish-white, of medium strength, lightweight and slightly spongy. It is used to build canoes, rural housing, plywood cores and tool handles. It is also used for shipping crates, match sticks, tongue depressors, toothpicks, veneers, gardening boxes, hay crates, boards, barrels and any other general carpentry. Its pulp is used for paper. Because of its exceptional three dimensional stability, it is highly recommended for kitchen cabinets, toys, rustic furniture and carved ornaments.

In Guatemala, this wood is also used as soles for sandals. It is not very resistant to insects, and its outdoor life is limited. As firewood, although light, it burns very well but is not dense enough to make good charcoal.

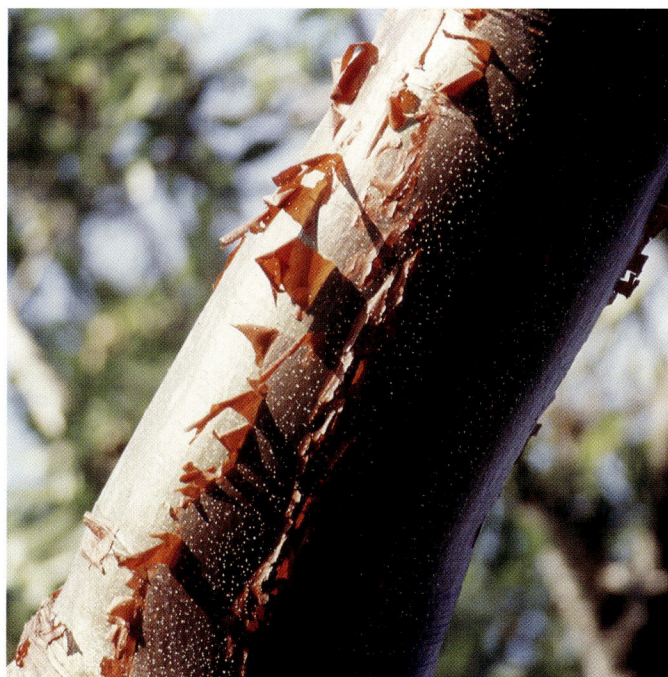

Bursera simaruba. Shiny red trunk.

SANTA MARÍA

(Lemonwood)

You inspire me with dark awe
with your furious growth,
Do you want to leave time behind,
consume life's surprises,
transfer death's borders and free her?
Oh, my land, rich and savage
Why do your trees
die so young?

Oh, I too was a tree in my land,
with precocious branches and flexible dreams
and when at last birds came
to celebrate my leaves,
on my frail branches
they could not hang their nests,
they could not sing their songs.

The Growth of Hurried Trees
César Brañas

Botanical name:

Calophyllum brasiliense Camb.

Family:

Clusiaceae

Synonyms:

Calophyllum antillanum Britton

Calophyllum rekoi Standl.

Common names:

Santa María, Barí, Leche María, Palo María, Leche de María, Palo María Blanco, Mario. Saint Mary's Tree, Lemonwood.

The Santa María in Traditional Lore:

Travelers from an exhausted Europe came to the New World in search of its beautiful natural resources and were favorably impressed upon seeing for the first time the lemonwood tree. Fray Francisco Ximénez, in "The Natural History of the Kingdom of Guatemala," describes this tree as possessing great medicinal qualities, including a certain yellow gum that accelerates wound healing.

In the "Flora of Guatemala," the Santa María tree is described as an important tree for its wood, especially those trees that are located in the Pacific hills. Today, this is not true, due to excessive clearing in large areas. However, lemonwood is widely used in the Izabal area of Guatemala for rural construction; and its presence is very important in maintaining the ecological balance in mangrove regions.

Description:

Lemonwood can grow up to 40 m tall and 1 m in diameter. This tree has a yellow latex. The bark is maroon, delicately fissured. Its wood is yellowish on the outside, and runs from pink to red on the inner layers, with a very fine and smooth grain. The wood has many exceptional qualities: it is compact, resistant, elastic, heavy and durable. The crown is very dense, small and well-rounded; and the tree is evergreen. The shiny deep green leaves are elliptical and have strongly defined lateral veins that run parallel to the central vein. The tree blooms in bunches of small, white, strongly perfumed flowers. The fruit has one round, green and yellow seed.

This tree can be found in southern Mexico, Central América and northern South América.

Ecological Requirements:

The lemonwood tree can adapt to rain forests as well as to dry or sandy soils. It can prosper from sea level to 1200 meters. If the soil is inadequate, the tree's growth will be hindered.

Propagation:

These trees reproduce by seed; the seeds sprout in two weeks and are collected in February. These seedlings must be tended for 5 months, ensuring they have enough light, but never direct sunlight. After these first 5 months they may be transplanted directly to soil.

Main Uses:

The wood of this tree is generally used for support beams, flooring, braces, ship's masts, crossbeams, bridges, tool handles, agricultural tools, truck beds, windmills and looms. It is impervious to termites and takes a long time to dry because of the resin present in the cellular spaces. The latex it produces is known as María's balsam and is commonly used for medicinal purposes. It speeds up the healing process after the removal of a newborn's umbilical cord. The oil extracted from the seeds can alleviate skin rashes, and may also be used in gas lamps. In some countries, lemonwood is a substitute for cedar wood and mahogany.

Calophyllum brasiliense. Tree.

SAUCO
(Elder)

A lot of it grows in those parts,
whence I understand
the plant was brought to Spain.
It is a very medicinal tree.

The Natural History of the Kingdom of Guatemala
Fray Francisco Ximénez

Botanical name:

Sambucus mexicana C. Presl ex DC.

Family:

Caprifoliaceae

Synonyms:

Aralia sololensis Donn.Sm.

Sambucus bipinnatus Schltdl. & Cham.

S. simpsonii Rehder

Common name:

Sauco, Sauco Colorado, Sauco Extranjero (Ostuntalco, Quetzaltenango), Sacstún (Alta Verapaz), Bahmán (Sololá, Huehuetenango), Tzolokquen (Suchitepéquez), Tzoloj, Tzolojche, Tzoljque (El Quiché). Elder.

The Sauco in Traditional Lore:

Elder grows abundantly in the Guatemalan highlands as well as in other regions. According to Jorge Luis Arriola, Sololá, the name officially bestowed on an Atitlán town in 1547 by the Oidor Juan Rogel, meant "Water of the Sauco Tree." The area had for many years previously been known as Tzolohá and Tzoloya, words from Kaqchikel, K'iche' and Tz'utujil languages, meaning the same.

Description:

The elder can be a bush or a small tree, about 3 to 5 m tall, with light brown or gray bark. The compound leaves have 5 to 7 leaflets; and the inflorescences form flat-topped clusters, 10 to 15 cm in diameter, with very fragrant white flowers. The fruits are small purplish-black, round berries that have from 3 to 5 seeds.

Sambucus mexicana is native to southern and central Mexico, but can also be found in Central América and in the southernmost part of the continent, as well as in the Dominican Republic and the lower states of the United States such as Georgia, Louisiana, Florida and Texas.

Ecological Requirements:

This species can be found from sea level up to 3000 meters. It requires a cool climate and fresh, deep soil.

Propagation:

As this species has sterile seeds, it can be propagated only by thick cuttings that should have at least two internodes.

Main Uses:

The wood from the trunk is hard and resistant, but the trees are always small and produce only short logs. It is used for building purposes, to make tool handles and for firewood. Elder is planted as a hedge, as a windbreak, or for shade. In Guatemala, farmers plant these trees combined with short life-cycle plants to take advantage of the green mulch produced when pruned.

The vitamin C rich fruit is used to prepare jams, candies, liquors and vinegars. Both fruit and flowers have several medicinal purposes. A tea of its flowers can be used to cure colds and as a sudorific.

The elder tree is usually planted close to homes as a hedge, or in the garden. It has no industrial use and is planted mainly as an ornamental tree.

Sambucus mexicana. Tree.

LIQUIDÁMBAR

Liquidambar trees abound in the Verapaz province, the
town of Rabinal to the mountains beyond.
It is a tree that grows greatly, and its trunk grows as
wide as a man's body. When you puncture the tree a gum
flows and soon becomes as thick and sticky as honey.
Its fragrance is so strong that it is worrisome.
It also is taken to Spain for many purposes.

The Natural History of the Kingdom of Guatemala
Fray Francisco Ximénez

Botanical name:

Liquidambar styraciflua L.

Family:

Hamamelidaceae

Synonyms:

Liquidambar macrophylla Oerst.

Common names:

Liquidámbar, Liquidambo, Bálsamo, Estoraque, Quiramba, Ocóm, Tzoté.
Liquidambar.

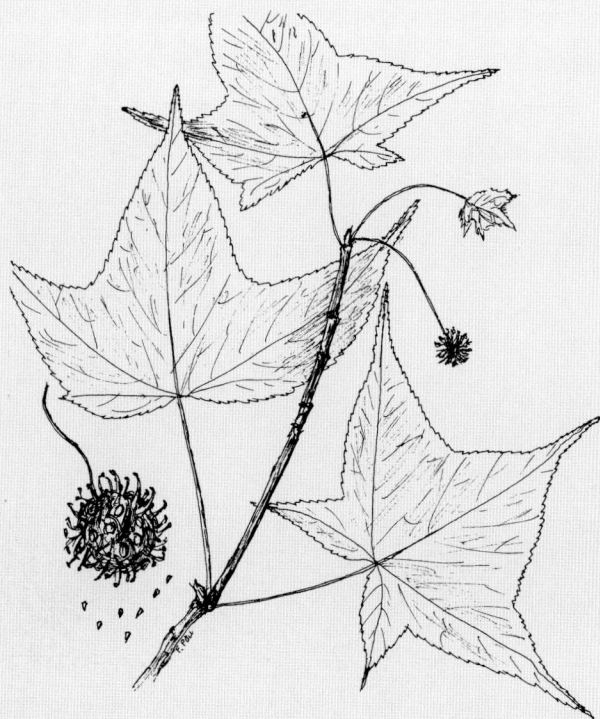

The Liquidámbar in Traditional Lore:

The resin or balsam obtained from this tree is yellowish. It hardens when exposed to air and has a peculiar odor, while its taste is acid and warm. According to Bernal Díaz del Castillo in his book, "The True and Extraordinary Tale of the Discovery and Conquest of New Spain and Guatemala" (La Verdadera y Notable Relación del Descubrimiento y Conquista de la Nueva España y Guatemala), in the pre-colonial era, liquidambar was used as incense in temples and homes; it was also used to flavor tobacco. The indigenous people of Guatemala chew the hardened resin to clean and 'preserve' their teeth. In Europe, the balsam is used for medicinal purposes; in Guatemala, to treat wounds.

Description:

The liquidambar tree grows up to 50 m tall in height and its trunk has a diameter of about one and a half meters. It may have extended roots at the base of its very straight and cylindrical trunk. The crown is semi-dense, very high and triangular in shape. The bark is gray and, in older trees, is deeply cracked. The leaves are bright green when young and red before falling. They have very long petioles and the leaf blades are finely serrated and palm shaped, formed of five to seven triangular lobes, not unlike maple leaves. The tiny flowers are grouped together in dense green inflorescences: the male flowers grow along the branches, the female flowers hang from the tree. The fruits are small nuts that hang in clusters two to three cm wide.

Ecological Requirements:

This species is naturally distributed from 900 meters up to 2500 meters above sea level. It prospers best at altitudes between 1000 to 1400 meters and within 12° to 18° C. The annual rainfall needed ranges from 1800 to 3500 mm. The tree grows equally well on mountain slopes as on the plains.

In Guatemala, liquidambar is found in: Alta Verapaz, Baja Verapaz, El Progreso, Izabal, Zacapa, Chiquimula, Quiché and Huehuetenango. Some specimens may be found in the capital city.

Propagation:

The liquidambar tree reproduces by seed. The seed, which needs no pre-sprouting treatment, is collected in April and May and usually sprouts within 12 to 15 days. It should remain in the nursery for five months before being planted to its final site.

Planting:

A distance of 3 x 3 meters should be observed when planting the tree, and the soil should be free of weeds, which liquidambar cannot tolerate. Preferably it should be planted between May and August, even September, but with a major risk of looses.

Production:

When the tree is from 2 to 3 years old, the wood is ideal for firewood; if used for construction- roofs, posts, etc., the tree should be at least 5 years old; if quality wood is needed, the tree should be from 10 to 12 years old.

Main Uses:

This wood is mainly used for fine carpentry and carving. It is used for cabinets, furniture, paneling, flooring and walls. The trunk produces a resin called balsam that is used to alleviate muscular and joint pain. Liquidambar wood can also be used as green firewood due to its high heating capacity; and the tree can be planted as an attractive hedge.

Liquidambar styraciflua. Red and bright green leaves.

GUAYACÁN

Valentín was now a brown Guayacán, hard as steel and of
excellent character. Even his manners had changed.
The restlessness of his temperament had become calmer, and
his ways slow, secure without haste. His look had lost its
feverish brightness and was now peaceful and tranquil in
spite of its hawklike or feline penetrability. He was changing
fast into yet another child of the forest, his spirit hardened by
its reverses, by the brutality and aggresive fierceness of the
Petén jungle. Like the Guayacán, which grows in the most
arid wildernesses of Guatemala, he needed this ambience to
develop in all his strength and wonderful quality.

Guayacán
Virgilio Rodríguez Macal

Botanical name:

Guaiacum sanctum L.

Family:

Zygophyllaceae

Synonyms:

Guaiacum guatemalense Planch. ex Rydb.

Common names:

Guayacán (Guatemala), Guayaco (Puerto Rico, Colombia), Palo Santo (Cuba, Venezuela), Zon (Maya). Lignum vitae, Iron tree, Tree of life.

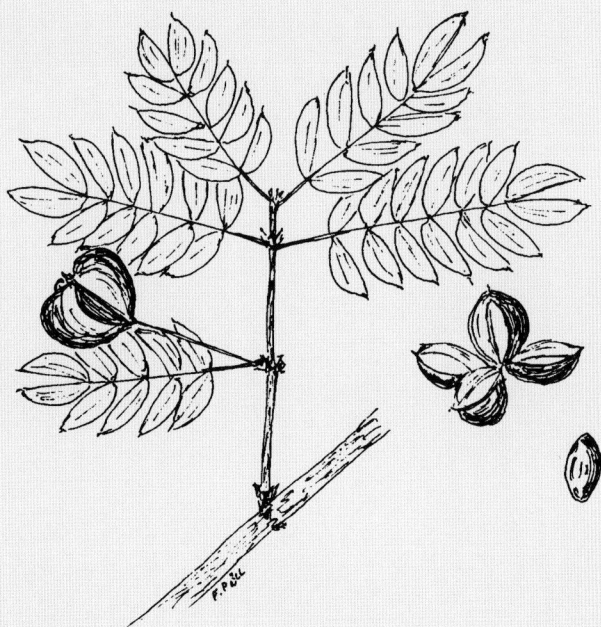

The Guayacán in Traditional Lore:

It is believed that "Guayacán" is a West Indian name, and that the tree does not have a Náhuatl name because it grows only near the coast.

These trees are extremely beautiful when in bloom at the end of the dry season (in the Motagua Valley, Guayacán blooms at the end of April), with a great quantity of blue blossom.

The Yucatán Maya used *Guaiacum* wood for making plates, cups, and bowls. The archaeologist Tozzer suggests that the Lacandones, even until recently, also made bowls from it.

Lignum vitae wood is olive brown, dark brown or almost black. It is oily or waxy, has a pleasant, sweet scent and its extract has a bitter flavor. The wood has been a commodity since it was first brought to Europe in 1508 for its medicinal properties. For a long time, it was considered a remedy for venereal diseases. Many scholarly articles about the properties of *Guaiacum* were published and its reputation as a curative plant was so firmly established that, for two centuries, its therapeutic value was never questioned. Now it is believed that Lignum vitae had little effect on the diseases it was supposed to cure. Nevertheless, the wood extract is listed in the U.S. pharmacopoeia and is described as having stimulating and diaphoretic properties.

Fray Francisco Ximénez wrote in 1722 that "the tree is abundant in this land, it is known to treat the Gallic illness (syphilis) and other pains, the wood is very hard and heavy and has a tinge of black."

Lignum vitae is suitable for tasks requiring dense, hard wood, and it stands up to wear and tear by friction. The wood of old trees is almost black in colour. These trees grow very slowly. Because of its hardness, Lignum vitae was exported and made into oarlocks for rowing boats during World War II. The wood extract and the resin were objects of significant commercial activity in Santo Domingo from the sixteenth until the beginning of the twentieth century. They were traded under the name "Lignum vitae." The Guatemalan writer, Virgilio Rodríguez Macal, immortalized this tree with his novel titled Guayacán.

Lignum vitae is cultivated and found wild in Southern Florida, Yucatán, El Salvador, Honduras, Nicaragua, Costa Rica, Panama, on the Caribbean Islands and in northern South América. In Guatemala, it grows in the dry, stony areas of Zacapa and Chiquimula and is also common on the plains of Suchitepéquez, Retalhuleu, the south coast, and in Petén.

Description:

The tree grows 5 to 10 m tall. It has a wide, dense crown and a rather short trunk that is rarely more than 30 cm in diameter. The bark is smooth and light gray; the composite leaves each have 4 to 12 leaflets. These are thick and somewhat glossy, between 2 and 5 centimeters long. The blue or purple flowers are solitary or in clusters. The fruits grow in yellow or orange capsules with 1 or 2 ovoid seeds inside. These dark brown or black seeds are covered by a red aril.

The wood is yellowish brown, dark brown or almost black whit fine texture and pronounced veins. This wood is dense, heavy and strong. The duramen, or heartwood, is resinous and very resistant to fungi and termites.

Ecological Requirements:

Lignum vitae requires a moderately humid to dry climate (between 750 and 1000 mm per year), although it survives dry periods. It grows at low elevations (250 meters above sea level and below). In Guatemala, the species is indicator of the tropical thorn scrub region, but it occurs in the dry forest as well. It prefers limey soils.

Propagation:

Trees are propagated by seed. One kilogram contains 20,000 seeds. The embryos are viable for only a month. Ripe fruits are gathered from June until September, and the seeds germinate within 3 weeks, but the tree is very slow growing.

Main Uses:

The extract and resin of Lignum vitae have numerous medicinal properties (they are stimulating, diaphoretic, laxative and diuretic). The resin is also used as an antioxidant for oils and fats, and in eastern Guatemala it is applied to aching teeth. A decoction of the bark is taken to treat stomach aches, and when this is consumed with plenty of hot water it relieves rheumatic pains. The wood is extremely hard and strong. Its firmness makes drying and working with the wood quite difficult. An air-dried board foot weighs five pounds, 4 ounces. *Guaiacum* wood lends itself to heavy construction, cabinetwork, coach making, parquetry, latching and crafts. It is used for making pulleys, wheel hubs, teeth on gearwheels, drumsticks, furniture, posts, bowling balls, rollers, spokes and cart wheels, hammers and crushers, tool handles, canes, chess pieces, bows, shafts and screw propellers of boats and submarines, and other parts of boats that are submerged in water. Branches and small pieces of *Guaiacum* can be used as firewood or made into high-quality charcoal. In addition to having numerous commercial applications, *G. sanctum* is an attractive ornamental tree.

Guaiacum sanctum. Flowers.

This wise heritage of the Maya, who knew nature profoundly, is not lost. It prevails in popular tradition and in the knowledge of 'curanderos' (healers), indigenous naturalist doctors. Nevertheless, systematic recording and in-depth investigation of this precious information is sadly lacking. In fact, it is at risk of being lost, as pharmaceutical interests and Western bias reach traditional isolated communities through the media. Curanderos are now very few, and it has been said that each one who dies is analagous to a library being burnt: the information is lost forever. There is an urgent need to explore, foster and store the infinite cures hidden in nature.

Other Uses

*Maya music has a ritual repetitiveness, and a sound and flavor
totally linked to nature. Its oldest tunes were borrowed from
the songs of birds: its instruments from the chants of Earth.*

Other Uses

Trees were utilized for many different purposes by the ancient Maya. As with the bread nut tree, the fast growing alder was systematically cultivated by the Maya. They planted it as wind breaks and used the composted leaves as fertilizer for their crops. The alder serves the same purposes today.

To protect the precious cacao plantations, the Maya planted cantés. For this reason, these trees are now called "Mother-of-Cacao" or Madrecacao in Spanish. The canté is one of the many trees mentioned in the Popol Vuh and has many different uses. The ancients obtained a yellow dye from its roots. Its flowers are edible and its leaves, medicinal. Its wood is extremely resistant, widely used in construction and carpentry. It also provides good firewood and charcoal. It is used to protect crops.

The Maya who lived near water bodies built canoes from different trees, depending on the region. They navigated the coasts and there is evidence that they reached distant civilizations to trade. The great city of Tikal in Petén was once surrounded by aqueducts. A theory sustains that these were used not only to supply water but as a rapid form of transportation through the jungle by means of calculated dikes and "shuttle" canoes. In Lake Izabal and the Río Dulce ("Sweet River"), both located in the Atlantic lowlands, canoes are carved from a single tree trunk; the huge conacaste is usually used for this purpose. The conacaste is also known as ear tree because of the curious shape of its seed pods. In breathtaking Lake Atitlán in the western highlands, the "cayucos" are built with boards of the avocado tree, extremely resistant to water and very common in the area.

The Maya processed the bark of the amate to make paper. Although they wrote many books, only three remain and their hieroglyphic writing is just beginning to be understood. Today, the amate is prolific throughout the country, and as with the ceiba, it is frequently found in central squares of towns and villages. In fact, Lake Amatitlán, located near Guatemala City, derives its name from "Place of the Amates."

Of all the arts, perhaps music best expresses the emotions and feelings of a culture. The Maya had elaborate performances of theater, dance and music. Music was also a basic part of their celebrations and rituals. Their instruments came directly from nature. They had -and still have- a variety of flutes and percussion instruments. Among these last is the "tun," a kind of drum carved from hormigo tree trunks. This tree receives its name from the ferocious ants that inhabit its wood ("hormiga" is "ant" in Spanish). It is ideal for musical instruments because of its deep resonance, and today hormigo is used to make marimbas. Although its native origin is still questionable, the marimba today is Guatemala's most characteristic musical expression and those made of hormigo are considered the best. The wood, leaves and seed pods of other trees become resonant drums, flutes, whistles and "maracas," as well as a diverse number of occidental instruments.

ALISO
(Alder)

Trees of my country...
Trees of the whole world...
Let it be my tender song and
brotherly embrace
that, in the name of all men,
today give you my heart.
Trees of the whole world:
conserve your bounty
forever and ever,
eternally.

"Salutation to the Trees"
Ramiro Antonio Paredes

Botanical name:

Alnus spp.

Family:

Betulaceae

Common names:

Aliso, Ilamo.
Alder.

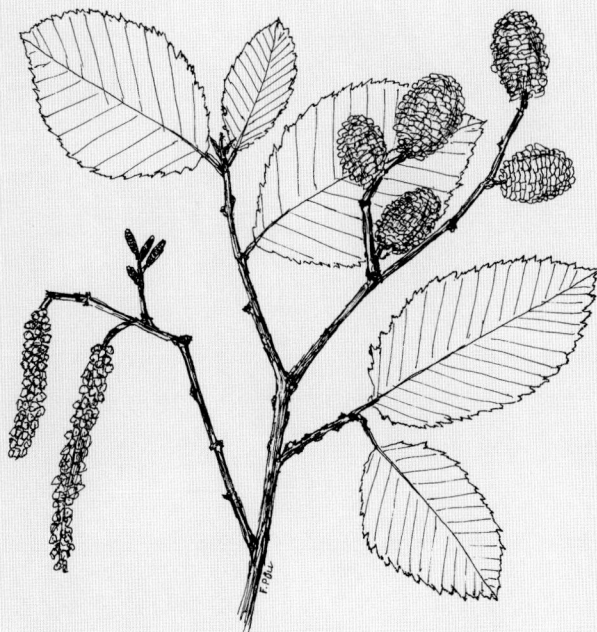

The Aliso in Traditional Lore:

Alder, well-known in all the Guatemala highlands, has a unique importance in the history of this region, being one of the first trees that the Maya used in agroforestry and later in silvipastoral projects (cultivation of trees associated with pasture for cattle). These systems, still maintained today, are excellent models for the development and management of more modern ones.

Currently, the alder is being studied with a view to its use, especially in agroforestry systems, associated with maize.

Description:

The alder is a medium sized tree, 10 to 25 m tall, with a trunk diameter between 20 and 25 cm. Its trunk is straight and cylindrical, its branches are thin, and the foliage is dark green. Its bark is thin and smooth or lightly wrinkled, with horizontal clefts, and is a clear to dark gray. Its leaves are simple, alternate and petiolate, oval, elliptical, with doubly serrated borders. The masculine flowers appear in elongated infloresences (catkins) and the female flowers are sessile or with short peduncles. The fruits are compressed nuts, generally winged, and are found inside the ripe cones, protected by scales. The root nodules fix atmospheric nitrogen by means of a symbiotic association with the fungus, *Actinomyces alnii*.

Ecological Requirements:

The alder grows from 1300 to 2800 m above sea level, with annual temperatures between 4° and 20° C, and annual precipitation between 1000 and 3000 mm with no more than 5 months drought. It needs well-drained soil and plenty of humidity. It is a pioneer species in secondary succession.

Propagation:

The alder reproduces by seeds. In a pound there are between 300,000 and 700,000. These have low viability if kept at environmental temperatures, but they can be maintained for several months if they are kept in cold rooms at 5° C. They are harvested from June to February. Pregerminative treatment is not necessary and the seeds germinate easily in 12 to 18 days. After 4 months in the nursery the plants can be transfered to a permanent location. In other countries propagation by cuttings has been successful; these should be from 15 to 20 cm long and from 1 to 2 cm in diameter.

Planting:

Planting varies depending on the system utilized and the objectives. Neverthless, for pure plantations, a distance of 2 x 3 x 2 m between the plants is recommended. It is very important to avoid shade during the initial tree growth period as the alder needs a lot of light.

Production:

The alder is a species of rapid growth and produces from 10 to 15 m^3 of lumber per hectare per year, with a good capacity for second growth which permits various crops to be harvested. For firewood it can be harvested after four years growth, and as lumber for construction after eight.

In the Flora of Guatemala the following species of the *Alnus* are reported:

Alnus acuminata Kunth
Alnus arguta (Schltdl.) Spach
Alnus ferruginea Kunth
Alnus firmifolia Fernald
Alnus jorullensis Kunth

Main Uses:

The alder is a multipurpose tree: it fixes atmospheric nitrogen, and the wood is used for the manufacture of jewel boxes and fine ornaments, firewood, construction and numerous other uses in agroforestal systems.

In the western highlands, the fallen leaves of this tree are commercialized for the elaboration of natural manure given its high nitrogen content.

Alder sp. Cones.

MADRECACAO
(Mother-of-Cacao)

They kept us in their midst as boys.
"Because of all this we will subdue them
and we will set an example."
They went along saying things like this
as they turned towards the base of the tree
that is called Canté.
They were accompanied by their older
brothers and they were firing the blow gun.
It wasn't possible to count the birds
which were singing in the tree
and their older brothers marvelled at seeing
so many birds.

Popol Vuh

Botanical name:

Gliricidia sepium (Jacq.) Kunth ex Walp.

Family:

Fabaceae (Leguminosae)

Synonyms:

Gliricidia maculata (Kunth) Walp.

G. maculata var. *multijuga* Michéli ex Donn.Sm.

Robinia maculata Kunth

Robinia sepium Jacq.

Common names:

Madrecacao, Calté, Mataratón (Mouse killer), Palo Negro (Black tree), Yaité (Quiché), Canté (Petén), Matasarna (itch killer), Cansim (Q'eqchi').

Mother-of-cacao, Quick stick, live fence post.

The Madrecacao in Traditional Lore:

"Mother-of-cacao," or *Gliricidia sepium*, is mentioned in the Popol Vuh and, according to the Motul dictionary, the Maya obtained a yellow substance from the roots of this tree. One of the best-known trees in many parts of Central América, it was given the name "mother-of-cacao" because of the age-old custom of planting it for shade on cacao plantations. Cacao trees grow better when they are planted in association with *Gliricidia sepium*, owing to the nitrogen-fixing bacteria that live in the roots of this tree.

Native to tropical América, the tree is found in almost all Guatemalan departments.

Description:

Gliricidia sepium is a medium-sized tree that rarely grows more than 10 to 15 m tall, with a spreading and sparse crown. The trunk is twisted and very branched and has a diameter of 40 cm or less. The light brown bark, is somewhat hard and wrinkled with white protuberances. While young, the branches are soft; later they become smooth. The leaves are pinnate with 7 to 17 oval or elliptical leaflets, green on top and light grayish green underneath. The flowers are light pink in color, up to 2 cm long, and grouped in clusters.

The pods, which are 10 to 15 cm long contain 3 to 8 flat, dark brown seeds. The wood is variegated with fine dark lines on a yellow ocher background. *Gliricidia sepium* wood is heavy, compact, strong and very resistant.

Ecological Requirements:

Gliricidia sepium is a species of hot tropical climates. It can be found anywhere from 0 to 1600 meters above sea level, but it grows better at elevations below 900 meters. It requires a humid climate with 800 to 2300 mm of rainfall per year and a dry season of 4 to 6 months. In terms of soil types, *Gliricidia sepium* is very adaptable, but prefers soils of medium texture. However, good growth has been observed in soils that are alkaline or rocky.

Gliricidia sepium does not thrive in very heavy (clayey), compact or swampy soils.

Propagation:

The number of seeds per kilogram is anywhere from 4,500 to 11,000. The seeds are gathered from February to May and can be stored for several years. They are planted in small plastic bags of soil at a depth of 1 to 2 cm. Germination takes place after 3 to 10 days. When the seedlings are 2 to 5 months old, they are ready to be transplanted to the field. Mother-of-cacao can also be easily propagated by stem cuttings. The cuttings are planted directly, at a depth of 20 to 40 cm. Under favorable conditions, a 90% success rate can be obtained. Failure of the cuttings to grow roots and survive is usually caused by long dry periods or compact soil.

The tree can be propagated by means of rooted cuttings, air layering, or direct field planting. The cuttings can be planted in containers in a nursery until they have grown roots and new buds, or, since *Gliricidia* grows roots very quickly, some of the younger branches can simply be cut and put directly into the ground. Seed-grown plants have deep roots, while plants that are propagated from cuttings have roots that grow near the surface. It is on the secondary superficial roots that *Rhizobium* bacteria fix atmospheric nitrogen (N) and improve soil fertility.

Planting:

The distance at which mother-of-cacao trees are planted from each other depends on the objectives the producer has in mind. Densities of 2,500 to 4,400 trees per hectare are recommended in order to maximize biomass, while densities of 1,100 to 2,500 trees per hectare are more suitable for the production of wood for products which can only be made from thicker stems. For hedges, one uses cuttings 1.5 to 2.8 meters long. These are planted 30 cm to 3 meters apart. For forage production, small trees are planted at a distance of 30 to 50 cm from each other, and 1 meter between rows.

For intercropping systems, a planting distance of 30 to 50 cm can be used between trees in a row, and 4 to 6 meters between alternate rows. The trees must be pruned regularly as the crop grows, and the trimmed branches and leaves can be incorporated into the soil.

A grid arrangement, where the plants in a row are 1 meter apart and the rows are 2 meters apart, is most suitable for reforestation and firewood production purposes.

Mother-of-cacao cuttings that have grown roots and new shoots are able to compete with weeds and require little maintenance. In poor soils, the tree responds well to fertilization with lime and super phosphate, which can double the forage yields.

Production:

Under favorable conditions, a hectare of *Gliricidia sepium* can yield up to 40 metric tons of leaves (fresh weight). Each tree can produce 30 to 70 kilograms of leaves per year. The production of timber or firewood varies with soil fertility; it may range from 20 to 40 cubic meters per hectare per year.

Main Uses:

One of the main uses of mother-of-cacao trees is in plantations, where they give shade to crops such as coffee, tea, cloves, and especially cacao. Its prevalence in cacao plantations gave *Gliricidia sepium* its common name, but it is also an excellent live support for black pepper, vanilla and yams. It is also used for hedges and firebreaks. The foliage is very beneficial as green manure or forage for cattle. The flowers are edible and the leaves have medicinal properties. The seeds and roots are effective rodenticides. *Gliricidia sepium* wood is very resistant to bacterial decomposition and insects attack. The wood is used for heavy construction, cabinetwork, furniture manufacture, crossties, sculptures, crafts, and shoemakers lasts. *Gliricidia sepium* is a good source of firewood and it is suitable for making charcoal.

AMATE

There are two types of amates; one has large leaves, not unlike a citron tree and the other has smaller leaves, as a lemon tree does. The smaller-leafed tree is called capul amate. Both bear a small figlike fruit that only the deer of the forest or the fish of the streams consume. This tree thrives along the shorelines of rivers close to uneven hills. And they grow and become quite large. They also spring from seeds that birds drop as they fly over; the roots grow from high up to way below, until they land on earth, and as they thicken and grow closer to other trees, they seem as one large tree. They complement each other as each tree springs forth from the other, such as a building comes from a stone. In the town of Cahabón, special trays are made from these roots.

The Natural History of the Kingdom of Guatemala
Fray Francisco Ximénez

Botanical name:

Ficus costaricana (Liebm.) Miq.

Family:

Moraceae

Synonyms:

Urostigma costaricanum Liebm.

Common names:

Amate, Higo, Matapalo, Cuxamate.

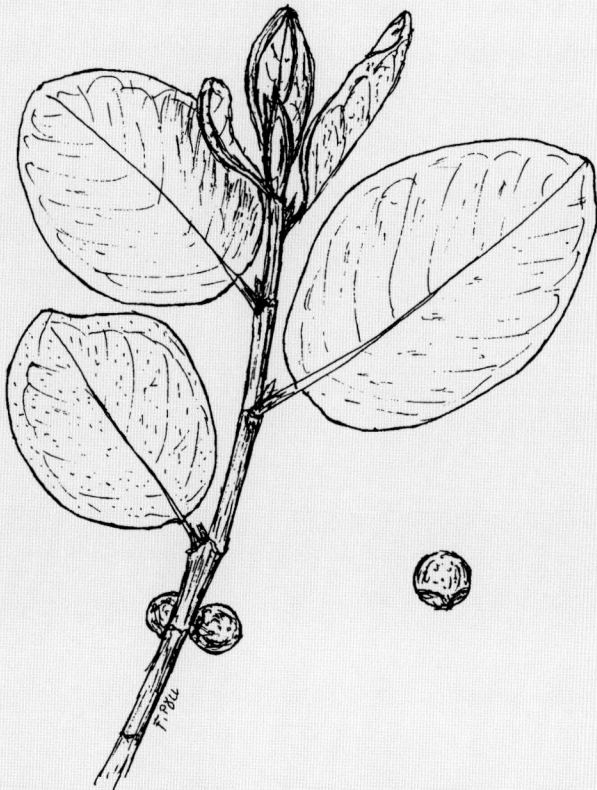

The Amate in Traditional Lore:

The name of this tree comes from the Náhuatl word "amatl" that means paper. According to Fuentes y Guzmán the term amate is formed by two words: amat paper, and tet stone, and placed together give birth to a new meaning for the word: stone paper. For as long as history records, amate bark has been used to make paper, and as written communication has been important in all cultures since the beginning of civilization, this tree has enjoyed special importance.

In the year 105 BC paper was invented in China. This invention traveled to Damascus and then on to Europe. To produce it the bark of the mulberry tree was used in China and "linen" fiber was used in Europe. Paper production was very important to the Mesoamerican cultures because their history was written upon it. The codices, true registers of incidents and the history of these ancient cultures, were written on amate bark and the bark of other warm climate plants.

The bark was also used to make ceremonial vestments and decorations. However, during and after the Spanish conquest, the production of bark paper lessened as the use of European paper only was authorized. The amate tree has a special place in Central American culture: it is commonly found close to homes, is a witness to everyday life, and is frequently mentioned in the literature of the area.

In Guatemala, there are around 33 native species of *Ficus*. *Ficus costaricana* is one of the more common species found in the central region, the Pacific plains and coastal areas. These trees can also be found planted along the avenues of Antigua and Amatitlán, and the name Amatitlán (a lake near Guatemala city) comes from the name of this tree, which is one of the loveliest in the country.

Many terms such as Amatl, Amate Gacho, Amatepeque, Amates, Amatillo, and Amatique indicate the close relationship between man and the amate.

Description:
The botanical name of the amate tree is *Ficus*. The tree is characterized for its milky sap, alternate leaves, both whole and petioled, and prominent stipules at the stem axis. In most cases the leaves fall. The flowers develop in a succulent receptacle, generally round, formed where the leaves join the stem. This receptacle has an opening at its end, ostiole, and is covered by small scales. These scales allow the pollination agents, in this case wasps, to enter separately within the receptacle.

The tree can be found in warm regions such as Izabal, Zacapa, Chiquimula, Jalapa, Santa Rosa, Escuintla, Guatemala, Sacatepéquez, Retalhuleu, Sololá and San Marcos. It also is observed in all of Central América. The tree is called higuero or higuillo in Honduras.

Ecological Requirements:
This is a shade tree, native to slopes and can be frequently seen along highways from sea level to above 2000 m. It is also planted along the shores of rivers and lakes.

Propagation:
The genus *Ficus* has from 600 to 800 species worldwide, which sub-divide into two groups: amates or higuerones that grow like any common tree, and the "tree killers" (matapalos or caimanes), semi-parasitic trees that grow over other trees, develop aerial roots and gradually strangle their host trees. The host tree will die and the *Ficus* is strong enough to continue alive on its own. Seeds germinate in organic matter that has accumulated in the branches of other trees. The *Ficus* tree is an important part of the food chain and birds and animals distribute its seeds in the tropical rain forest.

The tree is full-grown when twenty-five years old, and when adult produces large amounts of fruit (resembling a fig) and seeds. When these trees bloom and produce, birds and bats eat the fruits, excrete the seeds over other trees and those seeds that find the required conditions of humidity and temperature begin to sprout. Stem cuttings are usually used to propagate the tree. The cuttings, usually 50 cm high and 5 to 8 cm wide, are planted in moist areas, close to riverbeds, natural springs or ponds. Nurseries also use 30 cm high cuttings, and about 10 cm from the end, a small ring-shaped area of bark is peeled away carefully, not deep enough to arrive at the cambium level (growth tissue). A growth hormone is applied to aid root development, and the cutting is planted in a growbag or pot prepared with rich soil. When fully developed, the tree seems to be older than it really is because of its thick roots.

Main Uses:
Ficus lumber is very bland and has no commercial value. In forestry, the tree sustains the topsoil and retains mudslides due to its wide root radius. It is widely used as an ornamental tree because of its shiny stipules that decorate the random placement of roots and branches, distinguishing it from other trees. It is also used as a shade tree for livestock, and its fruit and leaves are used as fodder. The bark of younger trees, those 20 to 30 cm in diameter, is used to make paper. With a machete, a small incision is made at the base of the trunk, and the bark is stripped upward, uncovering the tree completely. Once completely stripped, the tree will die. Latex (milky sap) is harvested from several *Ficus* varieties and is used as a deworming agent.

PALO DE TINTA
(Logwood)

*This tree, also called the Campeche tree, grows
so much in América that there are forests of
it all along the Campeche coast. In Terminos
lake alone the enemy had felled so much that
in the harbor eleven boatloads of wood were
waiting, which the victorious Spanish seized
and from which they reaped great profits.*

The Natural History of the Kingdom of Guatemala
Fray Francisco Ximénez

Botanical name:

Haematoxylum campechianum L.

Family:

Caesalpiniaceae (Leguminosae)

Common names:

Palo de Tinta, Palo de Campeche
Logwood, Inkwood.

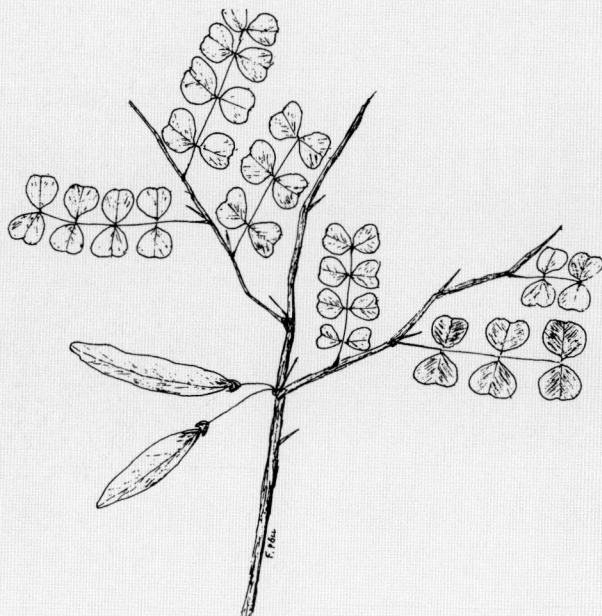

The Palo de Tinta in Traditional Lore:

Logwood, or inkwood, is one of the most important trees of the Yucatán peninsula and of northern and central Petén; in fact, the areas where the trees flourish are known as "inkwells" for, as the name implies, this tree produces a dye or tint. Native Mesoamericans traditionally used this to color their cotton cloth and other articles.

The Maya name for logwood is "ec" and the dye seems to have been used throughout the Maya area. After the Spanish Conquest, the use of logwood dye spread to Europe, but its use was limited as no fixative for the dye had yet been found. Consequently, England prohibited the logwood importation for over 100 years to protect British industry. During this period, however, a fixing process was discovered and logwood, or "blackwood," was clandestinely imported into England.

It was the search for and exploitation of logwood, together with that of mahogany, that sparked the British colonization of Belize. Originally, when ships left Campeche harbor to sail to Spain, pirates struck and seized the valuable bounty of wood. Later, they found it easier to depredate *in situ* the trees that grew near the coasts. At one time the price of the extracted dye in England reached 500 Pounds Sterling per ton, but in 1883 the price lowered to between 25 to 35 Pounds Sterling because of the chemical production of the dye. Small blocks of this wood are ubiquitous in Guatemalan market places, especially in Momostenango, where sale of logwood dye is closely linked to the tinting of the wool used to produce the textiles and blankets for which the region is famous. In western Petén, this wood is still used to make arrow shafts.

Description:

The usually twisted tree is about 8 meters high. Its bark is pale gray, its branches spread widely and are covered with thorns 1.5 cm long. The leaves have short petioles and are formed by two to four pairs of leaflets 1 to 3 cm long; they are finely veined, shiny on top and pale on the underside.

The flowers grow in dense bunches, full of thin and short-stemmed blooms. The fruit is 2 to 5 cm long and 8 to 12 cm wide.

Ecological Requirements:

Logwood grows abundantly in extensive marsh areas known as "tintales" (inkwells) in northern and central Petén, and northwest Alta Verapaz.

Propagation:

This tree has never been deliberately planted in a nursery; nevertheless, its germination has been observed to be an eight day process. Because of this, it spreads naturally with such ease that its cultivation in nurseries has never been necessary. The tree blooms in March and April and the seed can be collected in May and June. The tree can also be reproduced by cuttings, which has been the method most used in Guatemala. These cuttings should be at least two to three inches in diameter and one to one and a half meters long. The best time of the year for its planting is at the end of May.

Main Uses:

Logwood's main product is its compact, flexible and strong lumber. This resistant, long-lasting aromatic wood is whitish in its outer rings and bright red in its core. It is used for carving and paneling. The bark produces an aromatic sap widely used in varnish. The duramen (the inner section of the heartwood), the only commercial part of this tree, is bright red and it turns dark red when exposed. The sapwood (the softest part of a tree) is thin, white or yellow; its flavor is sweet and when fresh smells like violets. The lumber is strong, hard and heavy, and even though it can split easily,

it lasts a long time. Its specific gravity is around 1.00 and its weight is around 62 pounds per cubic foot. The finely textured grain is irregular and semi-woven and is hard to cut; it polishes easily and works well with fine finishes.

As already mentioned, this wood produces haematoxylin, a dye that is used on wool. It is also used in everyday dyes and those used for microscope slides. This peculiar dye when combined with boiling water forms an orange to red colored liquid that, when it begins to cool, gradually turns yellow and when treated, returns to its original color. If left alone, the dye turns black. Depending upon the acids with which it is mixed, different colors result; but the black tone, obtained by mixing iron-based materials, is most widely used. In the United States, the lumber is imported as small blocks that, when boiled, produce the dye (Commercial use of logwood declined because synthetic dyes replaced the natural product).

The tree also has medicinal purposes. In the United States it is a registered drug used as an astringent and in the treatment of dysentery and diarrhea. In Central América it is used for the same purposes.

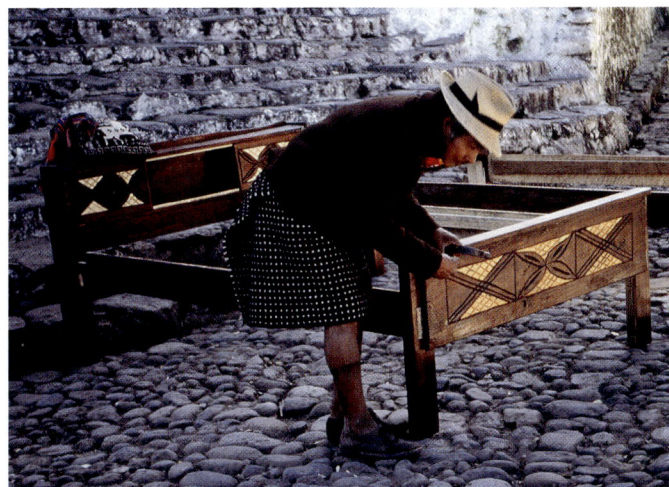

Nahualense man wearing a wool kilt (ponchito).

HORMIGO

The Hormigo tree
has its roots
very deep in the earth.
The warm and sincere earth
caressed by indigenous hands,
from which rise
all over the body
muscular strength
and sap of sweat.

The Hormigo tree
that stands as upright as man,
is lord of the forest
in whose branches
Jumbatz and Junchoguen swing
as happy children
and as withered old folk.
Jumbatz and Junchoguen
spring from branch to branch,
rocking themselves in the arms of the Hormigo.

My Song to the Eternal Marimba
Carlos Chinchilla Aguilar

Botanical name:

Platymiscium dimorphandrum Donn.Sm.

Family:

Fabaceae (Leguminosae)

Synonyms:

Platymiscium pinnatum (Jacq.) Dugand

Common names:

Hormigo, Cachimbo, Hormiguillo, Palo de Hormiga, Palo Marimba, Palo Marimbo.

Ant tree, Marimba tree.

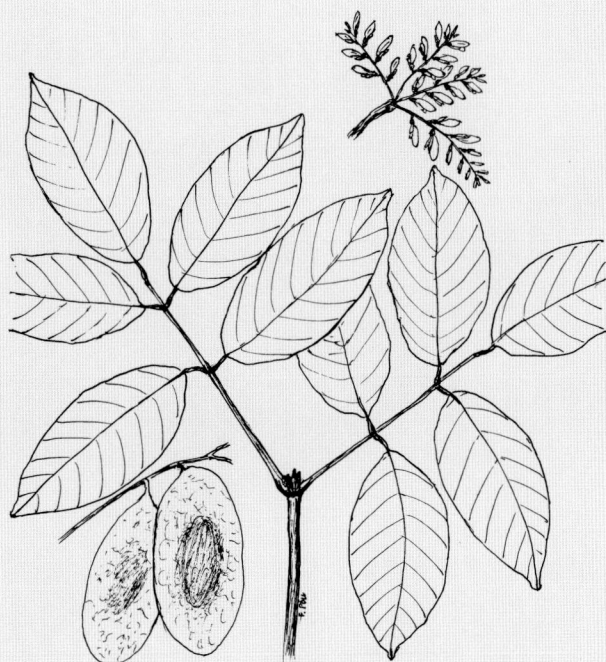

The Hormigo in Traditional Lore:

The importance of the hormigo tree in Guatemalan traditional lore derives from its use in traditional marimba production.

One of the most important characteristics of Guatemalan indigenous peoples is their music. Many of their instruments are still in use today: the chirimía, the marimba, whistles, flutes, drums, tortoise shells, rattles and the tun; and the one that is most widely used, even in ladino culture, is the marimba. The origin of this exquisite instrument can be found in the manuscripts of the sacred book of Teocalis, where a god plays the arm-held marimba.

The first marimba had only one keyboard, and later on gourds were added. These gourds were named bow gourds because they were fixed to the waist of the player with a strap and a bow. Later, bamboo rods were added and then four legs. This led to the substitution of the gourds with wooden chambers. The best marimbas must be made of a certain type of wood that produces perfect musical tones. This wood usually comes from the marimba tree or palo de hormigo but marimbas may also be made from passion fruit or rosewood lumber. Because of this ancient tradition, the importance of the hormigo tree is undeniable in the cultural development of Guatemala, and as an integral part of one of the national symbols of this country.

Hormigo trees may be observed in the Miguel Angel Asturias National Theater complex and in the areas surrounding the Hipódromo del Norte. These trees were planted by the Association of Guatemalan Authors and Composers.

Description:

The hormigo grows from 25 to 30 m tall, and its trunk is around 60 cm in diameter. Its trunk is straight, smooth and cylindrical. The bark is dark grayish brown, with long fissures. The wood is red with paler colors, fine grained, compact, strong, heavy and durable. The wood is resonant. The crown of the tree is sparse, and the leaves are odd-pinnate.

The three to five leaflets are long and dark green. The flowers are yellow and grow in bunches. The fruit is a small membranous pod, smooth and indehiscent, that contains only one seed. This tree can be found in Belize, El Salvador, Honduras and Guatemala. In Guatemala, the hormigo is found in Petén, Alta Verapaz, Baja Verapaz, Izabal, Chiquimula, Jutiapa, Escuintla, Suchitepéquez, Retalhuleu, Quetzaltenango and Huehuetenango.

Ecological Requirements:

This tree can prosper in mixed forests, both humid and dry, at an altitude up to 1400 meters above sea level. It is an indicator of the tropical rain forest.

Propagation:

The seeds are collected in March and April. The seeds sprout after 2 weeks to 45 days and should be transplanted in growbags when the plant has 2 or 3 leaves, and stay in the nursery until 4 months old when they may be permanently planted. The hormigo is a tree that regenerates easily.

Planting:

The trees should be planted 3 m apart. When young, the tree can resprout.

Production:

After 8 years the trunk will be about 20 cm in diameter and the tree can be commercially harvested.

If it is to be used for manufacturing musical instruments, the tree should be more mature, because greater age and trunk diameter provide more melodious sounds.

Main Uses:

The main hormigo product is wood, very red and well-known because of its unique resonance. It is not necessary to varnish the wood because it is naturally shiny and attractive. It dries quickly in the open air and very few natural defects result. The tree is usually inhabited by angry ants, hence its common name: the ant tree. Its main use is for making musical instruments, marimbas and violins, fine furniture, doorknobs, finely tooled artifacts, handles for home tools, rafters, parquet, and billard cues. It is also used in rural housing and as firewood, although it is not the best. Cattle love its leaves.

Traditional marimba.

PALO DE HULE
(Rubber Tree)

The Lords beckon you to come to play the ballgame with us,
So that we can rejoice when we see those whom we so admire.
Come then, say the Lords,
And bring the instruments needed for the game
the rings, the gloves, and also the rubber balls,
repeated the Lords.

Popol Vuh

Botanical name:

Castilla elastica Sessé ex Cerv.

Family:

Moraceae

Synonyms:

Castilla guatemalensis Pittier

C. gummifera Pittier

C. lactiflua O.F. Cook

Ficus gummifera Bertol.

Common names:

Palo de hule (El Salvador); Arbol de Hule (Mexico); Caucho (Spain); Hule, Hule silvestre, Ule (Guatemala, Honduras, Costa Rica); Cheel K'i'c (Pocomchi); Yaxha Kik (Lacandón); Kiirche (Q'eqchí); Uleule, Mastate banci (Panama); Caoutchouc (France).

Rubber Tree, Indian rubber.

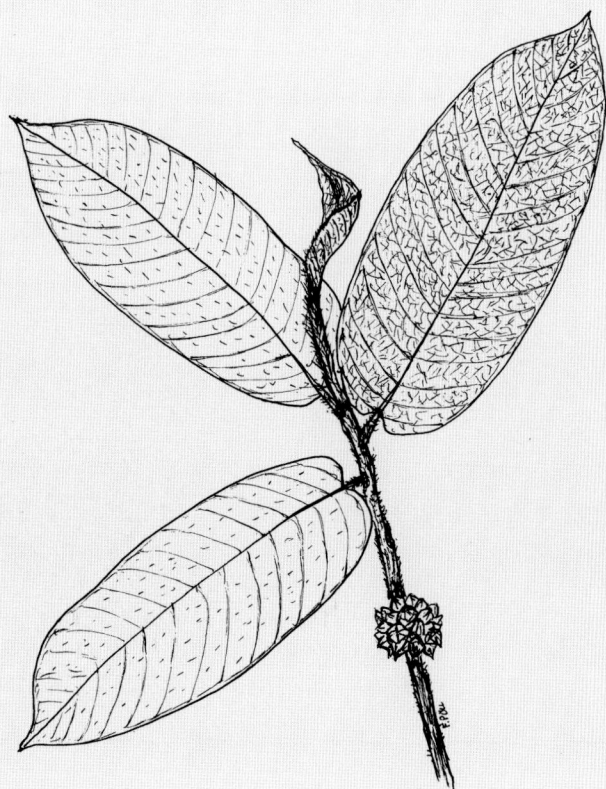

The Palo de Hule in Taditional Lore:

The harvesting and use of rubber was well-known to the Maya, as from it they made the balls used in their ritual games. These ballgames had a religious significance and were played in specially built plazas. There were different forms of playing the game in different areas of the country and also different sized balls, but it seems that in none of the games were the players allowed to touch the ball with their hands or feet, but must deflect it using hips, forearms, knees, shoulders and, in some cases, heavy stone yokes worn around the waist or, more comfortably, lightweight deflectors around the chest. The ball had to pass through stone rings, sometimes decorated with anthropomorphic figures, set high into the side-walls of the ball courts. The colonists in Mexico were probably the first Europeans to see rubber and introduced it into Spain. In Guatemala, the name of the river Ulapa means, "River of Rubber Trees."

Description:

The rubber tree is usually medium-sized, although it can grow up to 30 m tall and may have a trunk diameter of up to 60 centimeters. The bark may be either brown or light gray. The branches are densely covered with short yellowish or greenish-brown down. The branches are slightly whorled and are relatively slender. The treetop is round and will be wide when there is sufficient space; in a limited area, the crown will be tall and narrow. The leaves are large, simple and alternate, measuring from 20 to 45 cm long, and from 8 to 18 cm wide. They are opaque, dark green, slightly covered with down on the under side and display prominent veins. The stamens are on stalks in groups of 6, around 2 cm wide. The pistils are stemless, over 5 cm wide, and when ripe, are red or orange-red in color. The fruits are 2 cm long and 1 cm wide. The trees shed their leaves and also bloom during March and April.

Ecological Requirements:

The rubber tree grows best in humid or dry forests below 800 feet above sea level, but it will flourish in areas from 0 to 400 m above sea level, and at temperatures that can vary from warm to hot. It grows best in a warm, tropical rain forest or very humid, warm tropical forest. The tree is found naturally in the departments of Petén, Izabal, Alta Verapaz, Quiché, Escuintla, Quetzaltenango, Huehuetenango, San Marcos, Retalhuleu, Suchitepéquez, and Santa Rosa. The rubber tree can also be found in Belize, and from southern Mexico to Costa Rica.

Propagation:

The tree is usually planted by cuttings, similar to the amate tree. Given the great commercial success of the Brazilian *Hevea brasiliensis* rubber tree (of the Euphorbiaceae family) due to its enormous harvest of high grade latex, *Castilla elastica* Cervantes is not enthusiastically cultivated, though there are several plantations in Guatemala.

Main Uses:

This tree is known as a source of latex, an integral part of rubber. Even though this rubber was widely used years ago, today there are no commercial plantations of this species in Guatemala. All the rubber harvested from this species comes from natural, not cultivated, forests. The latex is used to make balls, bags, raincoats, and marimba drumsticks. The rubber produced from this species has never been exported in large quantities.

We have described this tree as mainly decorative; neverthless due to its extensive root system it should be planted far away from any buildings as its roots are so strong that they may invade and break the structure.

The palo de hule's wood is white, lightweight, solid and easy to cut. In ratio to its weight, it is relatively hard and strong, but not long lasting. In Guatemala nowadays it is little used except for decoration.

Castilla elastica. Flower.

SAN JUAN
(White Mahogany)

The earth sleeps dreaming of the stars,
but awakens remembering the mountains of yesterday,
that today are the bare hills of Ilom,
where the solitaire sings to the ravine, the hawk soars,
the termite hurries, the dove coos,
and on his rush-mat, sleeps his shadow and its wife,
he who should hack the eye-lids off those who fell the trees,
burn the lashes of those who fire the forest,
and freeze the bodies of those who
misdirect the water of the sleeping rivers, which see nothing
until unsuspected they
flow trapped into wells, where their eyes open and
comprehend all profoundly...

Hombres de Maíz
Miguel Angel Asturias

Botanical name:

Vochysia guatemalensis Donn.Sm.

Family:

Vochysiaceae

Synonyms:

Vochysia hondurensis Sprague

Common names:

San Juan, Sampedrano, Palo Bayo, Caoba Blanca, Sayuc, Robanchab, Yemeri, Emeri (Belize), Corpus, Corpo (Oaxaca), Chele (Nicaragua). White Mahogany.

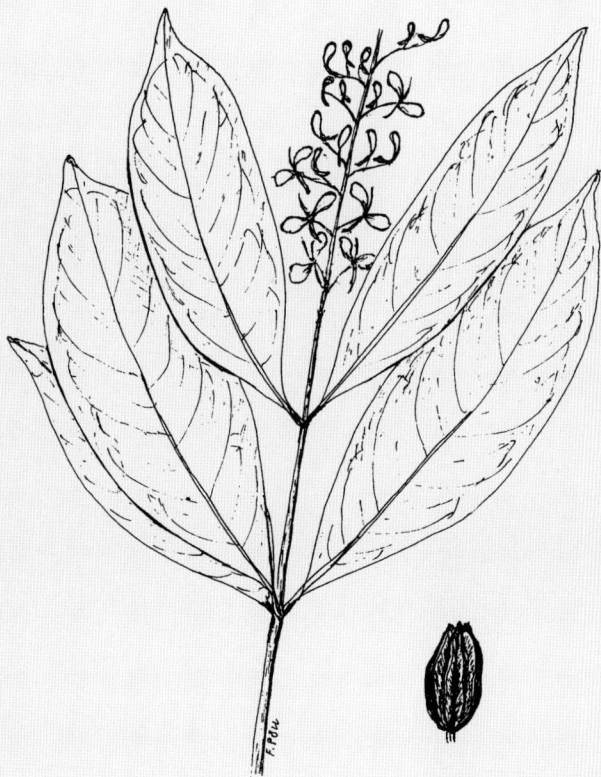

The San Juan in Traditional Lore:

San Juan is very abundant in the hills of the Quiriguá region and throughout the department of Izabal. It almost always projects above the tops of neighboring trees. *Vochysia guatemalensis* is very common near Puerto Barrios, Rio Dulce "Sweet River," and lake Izabal and has been used to build canoes. Propagation of this native species is desirable to enrich the areas where it grows naturally.

Description:

Vochysia grows to a height of 15 to 30 meters. The trunk has a diameter of approximately 50 centimeters. There are no branches on the lower two thirds of the stem. The bark is smooth and grayish, with rose-colored spots. The dense crown is round or drooping.

It has simple, verticillate leaves (arranged in a circle around the stem), in groups of 3 or 4, with slender petioles 1 to 2.5 cm long. The leaves are 8 to 15 cm long and 2.5 to 5 cm wide. They are bright green on the upper surface and darker green on the underside.

The bright yellow flowers have a soft, pleasant fragrance and grow in dense clusters. When in bloom, San Juan is very beautiful and visible from afar.

The fruits are thin capsules, 4.5 cm long and 1.5 cm wide. They have 3 deep grooves and appear angular and somewhat warty or fleshy.

The wood is reddish brown or light brown, with a rose-colored hue and a golden luster. It has a floury surface, a matte tone, and a rough texture. It is light and hard when dry. The wood retains its shape and stays in place if it has been properly worked. It has low resistance to the decaying actions of fungi and it is moderately resistant to termites. San Juan is a resiniferous tree.

It is also found in southern Petén, northern Alta Verapaz, Quiché, and in parts of Huehuetenango, as well as in Oaxaca, Belize, El Salvador, Honduras, Nicaragua and Costa Rica.

Ecological Requirements:

Vochysia guatemalensis grows in humid to very humid tropical forests, up to elevations of 700 meters above sea level. It is an indicator of the environmental conditions that exist in a very humid, warm tropical Life Zone. The trees prosper on coastal plains and in areas near rivers or other water sources. Preliminary trials carried out in Costa Rica indicate that the species' growth performance in alluvial soils (plains) is the same as in residual soils (slopes). It is an early pioneer in secondary forests, and can grow well on degraded rainforest soils.

Propagation:

White Mahogany trees begin flowering when 5 or 6 years old. They flower in May, and their fruit ripens in October and November. When the fruit opens, the seeds are dispersed by the wind, so the tree must be climbed before the fruit opens in order to gather the seeds. Approximately 1 kilogram of seeds per tree can be obtained. Another method of gathering seeds is to rake the ground below the trees. If the fruits are not quite ripe when they are collected, they should be exposed to fresh air in a shady place until they open. The seeds are easily dehydrated, and one hour of exposure to the sun will cause their germination rate to decrease from 80% to 59%. There is no established procedure for storing *Vochysia* seeds, but in a preliminary experiment carried out at CATIE, in Costa Rica, the seeds were stored in open paper bags at 30% humidity and at a temperature of 24 to 25 degrees Celsius. After 4 months, the germination rate of these seeds was still acceptable.

The seeds germinate 3 weeks after they have been started in the soil bed. Two weeks after germination occurs, the seedlings can be put into bags of soil, and after 5 to 7 months, they can be transplanted to the field.

Although there are fewer and fewer trees of this species every day, it is possible to obtain enough seeds for planting on a small scale because each tree produces a large quantity of seeds. The establishment of large plantations becomes difficult because the variations in quantities of seed produced from one year to the next and limited experience with seed storage methods.

Planting:

At this stage, the seedlings must be protected from direct sunlight to prevent burning. Planting distances of 3 meters by 3 meters are recommended. *Vochysia* is not a suitable tree for agroforestry systems because it produces excessive foliage and its shade is too dense.

Production:

The following yearly growth rates have been reported in Costa Rica: a 3.1 cm increase in trunk diameter, a 2.7 meter increase in height, and a volume production of 5.9 cubic meters per hectare. *Vochysia guatemalensis* drops some of its branches by itself (self-pruning). In plantations where plants are spaced 3 meters apart, this occurs for the first time when the trees are 4 or 5 years old.

So far, harmful insects have not been observed, but in nurseries crickets have been reported to sever young plants.

Main Uses:

The wood, White Mahogany's main product, is moderately easy to work. It is used for carpentry, cabinetwork, interior construction, veneer, and frame working. It is not suitable for turnery. It can be made into boats, paddles, barrels, chests, flat spoons and plywood. It is also used for fuel, and sawdust is a useful by-product.

Trees have many other uses. Some may have been lost in the jungles of the past; some have remained through time; some were imported during the last five hundred years. Maya culture continues to depend on trees in a broad variety of aspects. Guatemala has a long tradition with the forests that manifests itself in religion, in agriculture, in art, literature and architecture, in natural medicine, in carpentry and music, in daily life. The country itself is like the mythic Wacah Chan: its branches have different colors, different sounds, different flavors and odors, different powers; plentiful treescapes, each with its own special virtue.

The Special Place of Trees

Forests are the guardians of life. If we do not quickly understand the significance of the myriad forms of life that share these forests, they will be lost forever.

The Special Place of Trees

The special place that forests were always given is clearly reflected in the Mayan languages, with many names of places and people based on trees.

Sololá, the department where beautiful Lake Atitlán is located, means "Water of Sauco" or elder, a tree common to the area. K'iche' means "many trees", in reference to the rich forests of another highland region, populated mainly by the Maya nation of the same name. Kaqchikel comes from "Red Tree" and their capital Iximché was named after the bread nut, "Tree of Maize. Many towns are named directly after a tree, and there are numerous other linguistic examples. Guatemala itself is believed to come from the Mexican-Náhuatl etymology "Guauhitemala" or "Place of the Forests."The country lives up to its name. The National Forestry Institute of Guatemala identifies fourteen types of forests. Each region surprises with sudden changes, with trees that vary drastically in color and shape, with ecosystems ruled by their own spirits. Throughout the ages the Maya became an indivisible part of their diverse habitats. Their harmonic relationship and understanding of natural balance, and the urgent need to comprehend and apply their respectful ways, find a living metaphor in the mountains of Verapaz. This region, whose name means "True Peace," is home to the Resplendent Quetzal, national bird and symbol of freedom in Guatemala.

Identified with divinity and power, these birds were sacred to the ancient Maya. Maya kings used quetzal feathers on headdresses but never killed them. The quetzal once inhabited most of the Guatemalan highlands. Today, deforestation has drastically reduced its habitat, and it is now an endangered species. Young quetzals learn from their parents to feed from the fruit of the aguacatillo and this is their main nourishment. While the quetzal depends on the aguacatillo for food, the tree in turn depends on the quetzal for propagation. The sacred bird of the Maya -symbol of a nation- cannot live without the tree and the tree cannot live without the bird.

In the Américas, the forests of the Maya area are second only to those of the Amazon in oxygen production. They represent one of the most meaningful natural resources and they are essential to the daily life of the indigenous peoples and to the health of the planet. The Maya have always understood the symbiotic relationship between humankind and forests: an interdependence as strong as that of the quetzal and the aguacatillo. Trees of the Maya are reflected in their crafts, art, language, and beliefs. They are part of their existence and are used to cure their illnesses.

The Maya culture envisioned Earth with a mystic image: the sky sustained by branches; the ground held by roots. Both are united by means of the trunk to humans, animals, and flora that inhabit its surface. Everything has a meaning and a purpose. Everyone matters. All are absolutely necessary to create a world, the sacred Tree of Life.

GUARUMO

It would not take too long; in jungle life nothing lasts forever yet all is eternal... Life and death travel from tree to tree, they slither along the floor enveloped by it and even though everything dies, everything lives, everything feeds and continues.

La Mansión del Pájaro Serpiente
Virgilio Rodríguez Macal

Botanical name:

Cecropia obtusifolia Bertol.

Family:

Cecropiaceae

Synonyms:

Cecropia mexicana Hemsl.

C. mexicana var. *macrostachya* Donn.Sm.

Common names:

Guarumo (in the Cobán area, Guarumbo), Pacl, Choop (Cobán), Xobín (Baja Verapaz). Trumpet Tree.

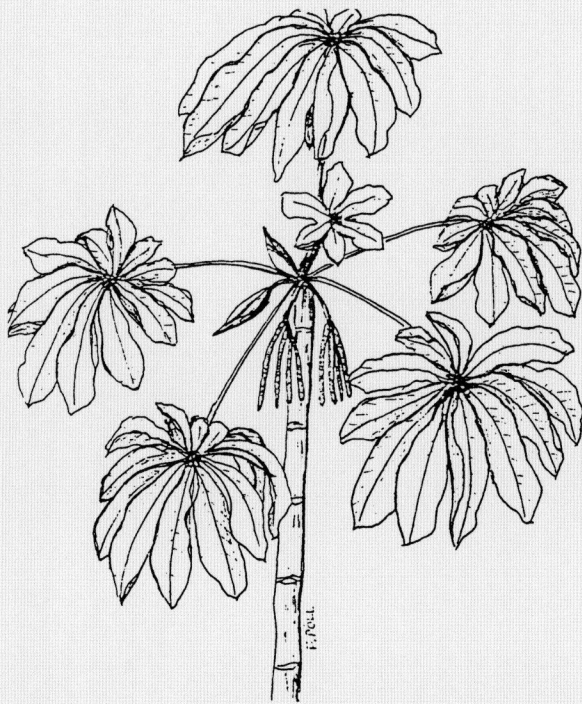

The Guarumo in Traditional Lore:

Quetzales and toucans feed on this tree, while black guans and chachalacas usually nest in it.

The common name of the tree is probably based on a San Marcos department dialect, but a Caribbean origin is possible. In Belize, it is called the trumpet tree because its stem has a hole in the center; however, Fernández de Oviedo called it "yaruma," a word perhaps closer to the original name.

Description:

The height of the trumpet tree can vary; it can grow up to 20 meters but is usually a low tree. The trunk is seldom more than 30 cm in diameter, sometimes with short and thick branchlets. The leaves have long petioles, with a leaf span from 30 to 50 cm. The leaf is divided into 10 to 13 lobes, green on the uppersurface and white on the underside. Male spikes are long and thin and 3 to 4 mm thick; female spikes 20 to 40 cm long and 6 to 7 mm thick.

Cecropia obtusifolia can be distinguished easily from *C. peltata* because in *C. obtusifolia* the female spikes are up to 40 cm long and in *C. peltata* the female spikes are only up to 6 cm long. The tree can bloom at 4 months of age; young leaves usually are red or purple although they are not always visible.

Growing naturally in the following areas: Alta Verapaz, Baja Verapaz, Izabal, Santa Rosa, Escuintla, Suchitepéquez, Retalhuleu, Sacatepéquez and Belize, *C. obtusifolia* has been transplanted from the coastal areas to the capital city and has survived and prospered. The tree can also be found in southern Mexico, Central América and Panama.

Ecological Requirements:

Cecropia obtusifolia usually grows in humid lowlands, swamps or rain forests. It is also used as a living fence in farms, grazing areas or forests from 0 to 1300 meters above sea level.

Propagation:

This species reproduces by itself, readily by seed. It has a good natural regeneration process if there is enough soil moisture.

Dr. Richard Fischer from Texas A & M University has indicated that although the trumpet tree invades fallow lands, it is difficult to reproduce in a plantation.

Main Uses:

The tree is used as a natural fence, the stems are used as support beams in huts, and the leaves are natural fodder for cattle.

A decoction made from young leaves is used as a diuretic, heart medicine, and febrifuge, and it can also alleviate bronchitis swelling and rheumatism.

Other Species:

Botanical name: *Cecropia peltata* L.
Family: Moraceae (Cecropiaceae)
Common names: Guarumo, Oxcochle, Ix-coch

Description:

Cecropia peltata can grow to 20 m tall. The leaves are dark green, rough to the touch and densely covered by white hairs on the underside. They are 30 to 50 cm wide and usually are made up of 7 to 9 lobes. The flowers bloom in spikes; the male spikes are 4 cm long and 3 mm thick, the female spikes are 3 to 6 cm long.

This is a native Guatemalan species, and can be observed in Zacapa, El Progreso, Chiquimula, Petén, Izabal and Santa Rosa. It also grows well in Yucatán, Belize, Central América, the Caribbean islands and northern South América.

Ecological Requirements:

This species can be found in the so-called subtropical dry forests, at 0 to 900 meters above sea level, with a mean annual temperature between 19 to 24° C, and an average of 855 millimeters of rain per year. It grows well in rocky places, or uncultivated land, be it moist or arid and along the roadside in recently cleared areas It is a pioneer species in secondary succession and grows rapidly. The seeds require high temperatures or fire for germination.

Main Uses:

The hollows stems are used for flutes and blowguns. In the Américas, these stems are used for horns and water pipes. The ripe fruit feeds quetzals, toucans, and crows. Its medicinal use is the same as for *C. obtusifolia*.

Cecropia obtusifolia. Trunk.

CHIPE
(Tree Fern)

"...This is not the first time, buds of humanity
carrying kindling, that you see hope rising from the soil,
your hope.
Hope for you can rise only from the soil..."

Meditations of a Bare Foot Indian
Messages of Torotumbo
Miguel Angel Asturias

Botanical name of genera:

Alsophila, Cyathea, Dicksonia, Trichipteris

Family:

Cyatheaceae

Common names:

Chipe, Chut, Helecho Macho.
Tree fern.

The Chipe in Traditional Lore:

Chipe is a tree fern, and due to its age of origin it can be considered a living fossil.

Description:

Its trunk may grow to 8 to 10 m tall; and its internal structure is woven with roots and the stems of old leaves. In very dense forests, chipe may grow up to 15 meters. Its leaves, or fronds, are complex and divided. There are no flowers or seeds, and reproduction is by spores. *Alsophila salvinii* Hook. is the only species that has both the petiole and the rachis completely smooth and black. It can be found mainly in the Verapaces, Chiquimula, Zacapa, Jalapa, El Quiché, Huehuetenango, Quetzaltenango, San Marcos, Suchitepequez and Izabal.

Ecological Requirements:

This plant can grow in areas from 1300 to 3200 meters above sea level, in dense and very humid mountain forests, in very rainy areas.

Propagation:

Chipe reproduces via spores; these spores form a thin green sheet, with masculine and feminine spores on it. Water is indispensable for fertilization, after which the zygote reproduces the fern.

Main Uses:

The trunk of chipe is used as a base to plant orchids, and it also is a decorative plant; but, unfortunately, due to depredation to supply these demands, this beautiful fern is in danger of extinction. In the Verapaces trunks are used as house supports.

Tree fern.

Fiddlehead of a tree fern.

Tree ferns in the forest.

AGUACATILLO

(Wild Avocado)

You emerge,
splendid burst of light and green,
from the lungs of the jungle.
Bird made of sunlight,
blood of volcanoes
and the burning desire
of our race.

Francisco Méndez

Botanical name:

Persea donnell-smithii Mez

Family:

Lauraceae

Synonyms:

Mutisiopersea donnell-smithii (Mez) Kosterm.

Common name:

Aguacatillo, Sacsi (K'ekchi').

Wild avocado.

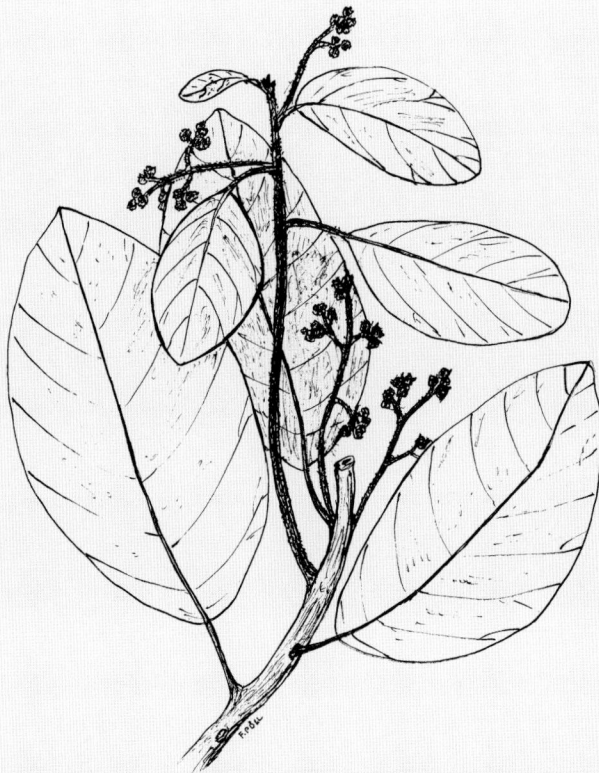

The Aguacatillo in Traditional Lore:

In Mesoamerican folklore the quetzal bird (*Pharomachrus mocinno mocinno*), has always been considered sacred. It feeds principally on the fruit of the aguacatillo, as do toucans, bats and cayayas (crested guans). Because it provides the main food source for the quetzal, which is the national bird of Guatemala and a traditional symbol of freedom as shown on the coat-of-arms of the republic, the significance of the symbiosis between the aguacatillo and the quetzal is deeply embedded in Guatemalan culture; hence the importance of propagating the tree.

Perhaps to perpetuate the bird's image, the official currency of Guatemala was established as the Quetzal during the government of José María Orellana, after which the parity of the Quetzal with the US Dollar lasted for more than sixty years.

Nowadays the quetzal bird is an endangered species as its habitat is constantly exploited. It still lives in a natural state in the Verapaz mountains, as well as in small and remote areas of the forests of Quiché, Suchitepéquez, Sololá and the Sierra de las Minas. However, it is no longer found in Sacatepéquez and Escuintla.

In Mayan times the spectacular feathers, or coverts, of the male quetzal decorated the headdresses of the elite, although the birds themselves were in no way harmed: for the Maya, the unique feathers and graceful flight of the birds were a source of admiration and respect.

Just as things of beauty are difficult to acquire, so is it difficult to observe the quetzal. A visit to the Verapaz area will not suffice; one must be armed with patience and health to scale the mountains of their habitat, at 1200 to 2600 meters. Then you may just see how their iridiscent feathers reflect the blue of the skies and the golden rays of the sun.

In the forests where it lives, the iridiscent green of its plumage blends perfectly into the perpetual green of its surroundings.

A large part of the quetzal's life is spent in the branches of the aguacatillos, oaks, pines or tree ferns, where wild orchids and bromeliads thicken the vegetation. Woodpeckers, hawks, toucans, chachas, owls, howler monkeys, raccoons, deer, tigers, foxes, armadillos, opossums, and porcupines also live in the same habitat. The decaying tree trunks are perfect nest areas; the quetzals also use abandoned nest holes of other birds and enlarge the area to be used.

From December to May the aguacatillo tree is in full fruit production. This is the time of year when it is easiest to glimpse this elusive bird because its feeding time lasts about 40 minutes per meal, three times a day. (7 a.m., 12 noon and 4 p.m.). In the months of January to July, the quetzal is in its mating season and will be seen from 1500 to 1700 meters above sea level. In August, the quetzal molts, regrows its tail feathers and returns to higher altitudes, from 1700 to 3500 meters above sea level. In the Sierra de las Minas mountain range, this behavior may vary; the quetzals have been seen to descend to lower elevations from February to June. It seems that the bird needs a periodical altitude migration to assure different habitats during the year. This is probably related to availability of food.

The aguacatillo fruit is small, and the quetzal eats it very carefully. It could be said that it takes its time and chooses the best fruit. It eats the fruit whole and defecates the seed. This is the process that defines the mutual benefits that the aguacatillo tree and the quetzal provide for each other. The bird feeds upon the fruit and spreads the seed, thus helping the repopulating of the tree. The bird also helps to maintain older forests, allowing the rebirth of damaged forests.

Description:

The aguacatillo tree is 5 to 12 m tall; the trunk is thick and its crown is low and quite dense. The newest branches are very twisted and are covered with a fine brown fuzz. The leaves are thick and leatherly, with thick petioles. The leaves are elongated ovals, almost orbs and are 10 to 20 centimeters long. Sometimes they are visibly asymmetrical at the base. The underside of the leaf is light brown, very twisted, has raised veins and is very visible from underneath. The numerous inflorescences are in the upper leaf axils with long peduncles and have sessile or short stalked flowers. Their sepals are unequal, the outer ones are smaller, the inner ones are widely oval, very twisted and persistent in fruit. The green fruits are tiny balls, around 1 centimeter in diameter when ripe.

The aguacatillo tree is found at Portezuelo and Sulín in Purulhá, Baja Verapaz, and in other areas of the municipality of Salamá and San Jerónimo, Baja Verapaz, as well as in many of the cloud forests.

Ecological Requirements:

The aguacatillo grows best at 1500 to 1800 meters above sea level in very humid cool climates. Its ideal medium is well-drained soil composed of sandy-clay, sandy-silty-clay, or deep sandy-silty clay.

In Guatemala, its growth occurs from the Santa Elena peak to Cobán, and on the Sierra de las Minas mountain range. The tree can also be found in Sololá and Suchitepequez and on the summits of the Quetzaltepeque, Chiquimula and Trifinio mountains on the borders of Guatemala with El Salvador and Honduras. In these areas reforestation is extremely important.

Propagation:

According to Professor Francisco Guzmán, the germinative capacity of the aguacatillo seed is best if the membrane that covers it is removed, and the embryonic end is planted downwards in the soil. This is why it is so important for the quetzal, the toucan and the bats to eat the fruits whole and defecate the seeds; it has been confirmed that a specific digestive enzyme of these birds contributes to the rupture and natural displacement of the seed-covers. The seed should be planted at least 5 centimeters deep, and at a distance of 15 to 20 centimeters. The germination period is around 28 days. When preserved, these seeds should be saved with the protective membrane on, in a dry and ventilated place, away from direct heat. They can be collected in January, February until early March.

Planting:

When the seedlings reach 10 to 15 cm tall, they should be transplanted to a nursery. After 10 to 15 days, they can be planted at their definitive site.

Main Uses:

This is a tree that grows in recently cleared fields; it is rarely used as a hedge, but can provide shade for cattle. It usually grows close to mountain peppers, pines, myrtles, blackberries, and trumpet trees. It can be used as firewood and fence posts, and is an important food source for animals, especially birds: the quetzal, the toucan, bats and the cayaya (crested guan). There is no set pattern for fruit development; because of this, the quetzal feeds on the fruits of the myrtle tree (*Myrica cerifera* L.), gooseberry tree, (*Prunus capuli* Cav.), trumpet tree, (*Cecropia obtusifolia* Bertol.), mountain zapote, (*Pouteria campechiana* (H.B.K.) Baehni) and blackberry (*Rubus adenatrichus* Schlecht).

There are several species that are known by the common name "Aguacatillo" (small aguacate: avocado) and can be found in regions where the quetzal has been found, for example:
Nectandra glabrescens Benth.
Nectandra sanguinea Rottb.
Nectandra sinuata Mez
Phoebe mexicana Meisn.

Persea donnell-smithii. Fruits.

The wise inhabitants of Guauhitemala,
Place of Forests, envisioned Earth with
a mystic image: the sky sustained by
branches; the ground, held by roots.
Both are united by means of the trunk
to humans, animals and flora that
inhabit Earth's surface. Everything has
a meaning and a purpose. Everyone
matters. All are essential to create the
world, the sacred Tree of Life.

GLOSSARY

All Saints Day: Celebration on the first day of November when people go to cementeries to adorn niches and mausoleums of their dead relatives.

Atol: Hot thick drink, usually sweet, most types are made with maize, but others include beans, rice, wheat or plantain.

Boj: Oatmeal cooked in water, milk and cinnamon.

Cachimbos: Name given in Brazil to the fruits produced by the Corozo palm in the form of large bunches of small coconuts.

Calabash tree: Name given to a tree in the Popol Vuh that narrates how the lord of darkness killed two great heroes and hung the head of one of them on a tree which was instantly covered with fruits.

Canté: Tree mentioned in the Popol Vuh. A yellow dye is obtained from its roots. The flowers are edible and the leaves are medicinal.

Cayuco: Name given to canoes used by native people in Guatemala.

Chachalacas: Birds of the family Cracidae. These are tropical and subtropical species of Central and South América. All are hunted for food.

Chée: Word for tree in several Maya languages.

Chilám Balám: Books from Yucatan which presented in the XIX century and contain important references of the Maya cosmology.

Chirimía, tun: Ethnic musical instruments

Chortíes: Ethnic group of Guatemala located in the eastern part of the country.

Concepción Chiquirichapa: Name of one of the municipalities in Quetzaltenango. Its Náhuatl form "chikilich-a-pan" means stream of cicadas.

Curanderos: Native doctors.

Day of the Faithful Deceased: Celebrations on 1st and 2nd of November when people go to cemeteries to leave flowers and offerings for their dead relatives.

Hun-Hunahpú: Name of the two main Gods or sacred heroes of the old Quiché kingdom. Hunahpú can be translated as blowpiper: hun, jun, one; and ahpup, ajpú, blowpiper. A character from the Sacred book of the Mayas, Popol Vuh. Hero twins, whose classical names are One-Ahaw and Yax-Balam.

Ixim: Word for maize in several Maya languages.

Iximchée: Word in several Maya languages (i.e. Cakchiquel) for the Ramon tree (*Brosimum alicastrum*).

Ixquic: Princess named in the Popol Vuh, mother of the twins Hun Ahpú and Xbalanqué.

Jícaras: Bowls obtained by cutting the calabash (*Crescentia cujete*) in half. The dry and hollow halves (jícaras) are used for serving drinks.

Jumbatz and Junchoguen: Also Hunbatz and Hunchouén, characters from the Popol Vuh. They were artists and musicians.

Kapok: Kind of cotton contained in the fruits of "cotton tree" (*Ceiba pentandra*). This product is popularly used in pillows, mattresses, life jackets and stuffing furniture.

Kaqchikel: Mayan language spoken by about half a million native people in Guatemala. Kaqchikel dialects differ in the number of phonemic vowels.

K'iche': One of the Maya languages spoken by over a million native people in Guatemala.

Ladino: Term used in Guatemala to refer to all non indigenous people.

Maracas, chinchines: Musical instruments made from calabashes previously dried and rid of the inner pulp.

Marimba: Name in Spanish for a wooden xylophone. In Guatemala it is usually made with Hormigo (*Platymiscium dimorphandrum*) wood.

Maya – K'iche': Ethnic group in Guatemala.

Mesoamérica: Mesoamérica was used by Paul Kirchhof in 1943 to define the region delimited in the XVI century by the river Sinaloa in the northwest of Mexico, the Coast of the Gulf (Lerma and Soto de la Marina); in the south, by the river Ulua in the Gulf of Honduras and Punta Arenas in Costa Rica. Though very diverse, it contains similar culture and history.

Mycorrhiza: Simbiotic relationship between the roots of a plant and the mycelium of a mushroom.

Motul dictionary: First Mayan-Spanish dictionary. The Motul dictionary was compiled in the last quarter of the sixteenth century, and on the evidence of his contemporaries, the author was Antonio de Ciudad Real, who has been called "the great Maya scholar of the century" (Ralph Roys, in Tozzer 1941:45).

Mulato: Person of mixed white and black parentage.

Náhuatl: Language spoken by one of the largest ethnic groups in Mexico. It was the official language of the Mexican Empire from before the XIV century until its fall, in 1521.

Nij: Insect that produces a wax used to varnish bowls called *jicaras* and maracas. It is used by Achi people in Guatemala.

Pacayas: Name given to the inflorescense of guano (*Sabal mexicana*) and *Chamaedorea* species. This edible when inmature and enclosed by the spathe. People eat pacayas cooked or fried. The name comes from the word **pakai**. The leaves are used to decorate churches and other places on Christmas Eve and festivals.

Ponchito: A wool kilt worn instead of pants by men of Nahualá, department of Sololá (nahualenses).

Popol Vuh: The Sacred Book of the Mayas.

Posol, pinolillo: Drink made of grilled maize flour mixed with water, sugar and cocoa.

Pseudo-cuttings: Are cuttings with a short segment of stump attached. Vegetative propagation with pseudocuttings is also possible.

Shilote: The dry husk left after removing the corn grains.

Sololá: One of the 22 departments into which Guatemala is divided and also the name of one of the municipalities.

Tinta: Spanish word for ink. The Maya obtained ink from the Logwood or Ink Tree to dye cotton and other materials.

Tortilla: Thin flat Mesoamerican maize cake eaten hot.

Tzicozapotl: Náhuatl name from which the Spanish name (Chicozapote) is derived. The English name is gum zapote or gum sapodilla.

Tzité or Ajsite: Queqchí term for the sorcerers or medicine men who make magic ointments with the seeds of *Erythrina*.

Tzutuhil: One of the ethnic groups in Guatemala and also the name of their language. They are located in the south-western part of Lake Atitlan.

Wacah Cham: Mystic symbol of the Mayas. They conceived creation as a marvelous tree, so the Wacah Cham was the "Tree of Life" and the column that sustained the universe.

Xibalbá: Underground region inhabited by man's enemies. The Mayas called Xibalbá to Hell and it was the lowest part of the Tree of Life.

Xiote, Jiote: In old castellano the "J" was written as "X". Xiote and Jiote are the same word.

BIBLIOGRAPHY

Aguilar C., J.M. 1980. Código oficial para las especies arbóreas de Guatemala. INTECAP-INAFOR.

Aguilar, José María. 1983. Catálogo ilustrado de los Árboles de Guatemala. Industria Gráfica Guatemalteca. Vol. I. 250 pp.

Aguilar C., Jose María; Aguilar C. Marco Antonio. 1992. Árboles de la Biosfera Maya, Petén. Centro de Estudios Conservacionistas (CECON), Escuela de Biología, Guatemala. 272 pp.

Aguilar C., Marco A. y J.L. Aguilar G. 1966. *Abies guatemalensis* Rehnder, Pinabete, especie arbórea digna de conservarse; 2a. edición. Guatemala. 383 pp.

Aragón Barrios, U.R. 1990. Caracterización preliminar del Ramón (*Brosimum alicastrum* Swartz), in situ, en el bosque muy húmedo subtropical cálido de Petén, Guatemala. Tesis USAC, Fac. Agronomía.

Arriola, Jorge Luis. 1973. El Libro de las Geonimias de Guatemala. Seminario de Integración Económica, Diccionario Etimológico. Editorial José de Pineda Ibarra. 710 pp.

Asturias, Miguel Angel. 1987. Hombres de Maíz. Edit. Piedra Santa, Guatemala. 275 pp.

Baer, P. y W. Merrifield. 1981. Los Lacandones de México. Dos estudios. 2a. ed. Instituto Nacional Indigenista, México.

Benítez , R.F. y J.L. Montesinos. 1988. Catálogo de 100 especies forestales de Honduras. Escuela Nacional de Ciencias Forestales, Honduras. 216 pp.

Boremanse, Didier. 1981. Final Link with Maya Indians. Geographical Magazine. Vol. LIII. (4): 250-256.

Boremanse, Didier. 1981. Los Lacandones. Revista GeoMundo.Vol 5 (5): 433-447.

Coe, M.D. and S.D. Coe. 1996. The True History of Chocolate. Thames & Hudson, New York. 280 pp.

Coe, M.D. 1992. Breaking the Maya Code. Thames & Hudson. New York, U.S.A. 304 pp.

CATIE. 1986. Silvicultura de especies promisorias para producción de leña en América Central, resultados de cinco años de investigación. Costa Rica. 228 pp.

CATIE. 1991. Madrecacao (*Gliricidia sepium*). Especie de árbol de uso múltiple en América Central. Colección de Guías Silviculturales. No. 7. Costa Rica. 59 pp.

CATIE. 1991. Ciprés (*Cupressus lusitanica*) Especie de árbol de uso múltiple en América Central. Colección de Guías Silviculturales. No. 8. Costa Rica. 66 pp.

CATIE. 1991. Leucaena (*Leucaena leucocephala* Lam. De Wit) Especie de árbol de uso múltiple en América Central. Colección de Guías Silviculturales No. 14. Costa Rica. 60 pp.

CATIE. 1991. Pino caribe (*Pinus caribaea*) Especie de árbol de uso múltiple en América Central. Colección de Guías Silviculturales No. 8. Costa Rica. 59 pp.

DIGEBOS. 1991. Tratamientos pregerminativos de semillas forestales. Documento mimeografiado. Banco de semillas forestales. Guatemala.

Echenique, Ramón. 1970. Descripción, características y usos de 25 maderas tropicales mexicanas. Cámara Nacional de la Industria de la Construcción, México. 237 pp.

INAFOR. 1977. El Chut o chipe en las montañas de Baja Verapaz. Guatemala. Copia mimeografiada. 22 pp.

Fish and Wildlife Service, Department of the Interior. 1979. Determination that *Abies guatemalensis* is a threatened Species. Federal Register. Part II. Vol. 2 (218).

Flores Arzú, Roberto. 1991. Estudio reproductivo y etnobotánico del Esquisúchil, *Bourreria huanita* (Llave & Lex) Hemsl., Boraginaceae; en la Antigua Guatemala Pueblos Vecinos. Tesis. Licenciado en Ciencias Químicas y Farmacia. Guatemala. Facultad de Ciencias Químicas y Farmacia. Universidad de San Carlos de Guatemala. 95 pp.

Gibson, Dorothy N. 1970. Boraginaceae. In Flora of Guatemala. Fieldiana, Bot. 24 (9).

González M., J.H. y C. Castañeda. 1983. Las comunidades de Pinabete en Guatemala. TIKALIA. Vol. 2 (1). Editorial Universitaria FAUSAC. USAC. Guatemala. 81 pp.

INAFOR. 1990. Calendario de fructificación de algunas especies forestales de Guatemala. INAFOR. Guatemala.

Instituto Nicaraguense de Recursos Naturales y del Ambiente (IRENA). 1992. Arboles Forestales Útiles para su Propagación. IRENA, Managua, Nicaragua. 267 pp.

Luján Muñoz, Luis y R. Toledo Palomo. 1986. Jícaras y Guacales en la Cultura Mesoamericana. Guatemala. Subcentro Regional de Artesanías y Artes Populares.

Martínez, Héctor. 1985. Sistemas Agroforestales. Memoria de cursos. Proyecto Leña y Fuentes Alternas de Energía. CATIE-INAFOR, Guatemala. 136 pp.

Martínez, Héctor. 1985. Viveros para producción de leña. Memoria de cursos. Proyecto Leña y Fuentes Alternas de Energía. CATIE-INAFOR, Guatemala. 136 pp.

Monteforte Toledo, Mario. 1989. Las Formas y los Días del Barroco en Guatemala. Turner Libros, S.A, España.

Morley, Sylvanus G. 1956. La Civilización Maya. 2a. edición. Fondo de Cultura Económica, México. 575 pp.

Nash, Dorothy L. 1976. Caprifoliaceae. In Flora of Guatemala. Fieldiana, Bot. 24 (11).

NAS-CATIE. 1984. Especies para leña: arbustos y árboles para la producción de energía. NAS. CATIE, Costa Rica. 344 pp.

Nichols, D. y E., González. 1992. Especies Nativas y Exóticas para la reforestación en la zona sur de Costa Rica. Oficina de Publicaciones de la UNED, Costa Rica. 84 pp.

Niembro Rocas, A. 1986. Árboles y arbustos útiles de México. Universidad Autónoma Chapingo. LIMUSA, México. 206 pp.

Ochse, J., M.J., Soule Jr., M.J. Dijkman y C. Wehlburg. 1980. Cultivo y mejoramiento de plantas tropicales y subtropicales. Vol. I. Editorial LIMUSA, México. 828 pp.

Padilla Quiroa, Francisco. 1987. Manual Práctico de Viveros Forestales. Proyecto Madeleña, INAFOR - CATIE. Guatemala.

Polonsky Célcer, Enrique. 1962. Monografía Antológica del Árbol. Editorial José Pineda Ibarra, Guatemala. 333 pp.

Puleston, D.E. y P.O. Puleston. 1986. El Ramón como base de la dieta alimenticia de los antiguos mayas de Tikal (nuevos datos sobre subsistencia alimenticia en el Maya Clásico) Informe presentado a la trigésima tercer reunión de la Sociedad de Arqueología Americana. USA.

Recinos, A. 1986. Popol Vuh. Las Antiguas historias del Quiché. Editorial Piedra Santa, Guatemala. 187 pp.

Rodríguez Macal, Virgilio. 1969. Guayacán./ Virgilio Rodríguez Macal. Guatemala: Editorial Piedra Santa. 560 pp.

Rubio, J. Francisco. 1987. El árbol en la poesía guatemalteca /J. Francisco Rubio. Guatemala: Editorial Jose Pineda Ibarra. 441 pp.

Saravia R., Milton E. 1990. Cultivos Tradicionales de Exportación. Facultad de Ciencias Agrícolas, Universidad Rafael Landívar, Guatemala. 244 pp.

Schele, Linda. 1990. A Forest of Kings: The Untold Story of Ancient Maya. Linda Schele & David Freidel. New York: William Morrow & Co. Inc. 542 pp. Ilustr.

Standley, P.C. & Steyermark, J.A. 1958. Cupressaceae, Pinaceae, Palmae. In Flora of Guatemala. Fieldiana, Bot. 24 (1).

Standley, P.C. & Steyermark, J.A.1952. Betulaceae, Fagaceae. In Flora of Guatemala. Fieldiana, Bot. 24 (3).

Standley , PC. & Steyermark, J.A., 1946. Moraceae. Lauraceae, Hamamelidaceae. In Flora of Guatemala. Fieldiana, Bot. 24 (4).

Standley, P.C. & Steyermark, J.A., 1946. Leguminosae, Burseraceae, Malpighiaceae. Meliaceae Zygophyllaceae. In Flora of Guatemala. Fieldiana, Bot. 24 (5).

Standley, P.C. & Steyermark, J.A. 1949. Bombacaceae, Sterculiaceae., Vochysiaceae. In Flora of Guatemala. Fieldiana, Bot. 24 (6).

Standley, P.C. & Louis O. Williams. 1961. Guttiferae, Rhizophoraceae. In Flora of Guatemala. Fieldiana, Bot. 24 (7).

Standley, P.C. & Louis O. Williams, 1966. Sapotaceae. In Flora of Guatemala. Fieldiana, Bot. 24 (8).

Standley, P.C. & Louis O. Williams, 1974. Bignoniaceae. In Flora of Guatemala. Fieldiana, Bot. 24 (10).

Stephens, John. L. 1969. Incidents of Travel in Central América, Chiapas and Yucatán. Volume I. Dover Publications, Inc., New York,. 424 pp.

Tedlock, D. 1996. Popol Vuh. Simon & Schuster, New York. 388 pp.

USAC-DIGI. 1989. Especies vegetales de uso actual y potencial en alimentación y medicina de las zonas semiáridas del nororiente de Guatemala. Cuadernos de Investigación, Dirección General de Investigación. Guatemala.

USAC-CECON. 1992. Deondrología Tropical, manual para guarda recursos. USAC-CECON. Fundación Mario Dary. Guatemala. 163 pp.

Valle Dawson, C.H. 1979. Vademecun forestal. INTECAP, Guatemala.

Vega, L.E. 1978. Crecimiento del Cedro, Cedrela odorata manejado en fajas de rastrojo y en el asocio inicial con cultivos, San José de Guaviare, Colombia. CONIF. 19 pp.

Ximénez, Francisco. 1967. Historia Natural del Reino de Guatemala. Ed. José Pineda Ibarra, Guatemala. 351 pp.

Young, Kenneth R. 1980. Guía de árboles para viveros forestales. Instituto Nacional Forestal, Guatemala. 200 pp.

INDEX

The accepted names for species are in [bold] roman type. Common names are in roman type. Taxonomic synonyms and other accepted species casually mentioned in the text are in [italics].